Get used to different

Have you found a spotless lamb for sacrifice?
-Pharisee to the Shepherd, Pilot Ep.

That's not for you.
-Jesus to Mary Magdalene, Ep. 1

I was one way and now I'm completely different.
-Mary Magdalene to Nicodemus, Ep. 2

I hope my next students ask the same questions you do.
-Jesus to the children, Ep. 3

You have much bigger things ahead of you.
-Jesus to Simon, Ep. 4

If not now, when?
-Mother Mary to Jesus, Ep. 5

Please don't turn away from me.
-Leper to Jesus, Ep. 6

Everything I thought I knew, what if it's wrong?
-Matthew to his mother, Ep. 7

It would be good if you believed me.
-Jesus to the Samaritan woman, Ep. 8

The Chosen Study

Water for the Thirsty

The Chosen Study
Water for the Thirsty

A welcoming and
Interactive experience for everyone:
observers... skeptics... learners... seekers... followers.

The Chosen Study Team

Bill & Teresa Syrios, Dietrich Gruen,
Tori Foss, Bill Ditewig and Don & Cathy Baker

TheChosenStudy.org
Watch > Discover > Relate
the Most Audacious
Story ever told.

If anyone thirsts, let him come to me and drink.
-Jesus (John 7:37)

Crossover Press

©2022 The Chosen Study: Season One, Bill Syrios & TCS Team
Scripture quotations are from the ESV® Bible (The Holy Bible, English Standard Version®), ©2001 by Crossway, a publishing ministry of Good News Publishers. Used by permission. All rights reserved.

The Chosen Study is not affiliated with *The Chosen* TV show or *Angel Studios.* Thanks to Michael Foster for his help with the *Realistic But Real?* and *Knowing Those Who Knew Him Best* sections.

ISBN: 978-0-9716683-3-1

"**The Chosen** is a television drama based on the life of Jesus Christ, created, directed and co-written by American filmmaker, Dallas Jenkins. It is the first multi-season series about the life of Christ, and season one was the highest crowd-funded TV series or film project of all time.

The series' creators stated that they had hoped to distinguish the new series from previous portrayals of Jesus by crafting a multi-season, episode-based story. The series portrays Jesus 'through the eyes of those who met him.'"   –*The Chosen*, Wikipedia

The Chosen Study focuses on *filling out* the series with Scripture passages to take everyone deeper. The guide can profitably be used by individuals with the hope that they... we... facilitate outreach and learning with others in one-on-one and group contexts. After all: *People must know!*

Contents

Welcome to The Chosen Study: Season One

Like the man himself, the accounts of Jesus' life and ministry are unique in the field of literature. Ancient writings include historical accounts, personal memoirs, and mythological stories. But none of these styles describe how Matthew, Mark, Luke, and John wrote.

They combine the roles of historian, biographer, theologian, and pastor. These "reporters" are not simply neutral observers but men who had been deeply influenced by the message they desired to communicate. Lacking literary precedent, second-century Christians called them *Evangelists,* and their writings, *The Gospels.*

The English word "gospel" comes from the Greek term, *evangelion,* which means "good news." The four Evangelists wanted their readers to not only know how remarkable Jesus was, but to know how good his message becomes in the lives of those who embrace it.

To understand that message better, we have selected key Bible passages portrayed in *The Chosen.* So, wherever you may be spiritually— an **observer... skeptic... learner... seeker... or follower**—we are glad you've joined us to learn from those who knew Jesus best.

Bible Study 2.0 = Food + Film + Scripture + Discussion

The Chosen Study includes ten studies. We typically:

-**Meet weekly** to watch>discover>relate and to develop friendships.

-**Start with a meal**, potluck, or finger food to relax with each other.

-**Have no need** to bring Bibles. This guide includes all Scripture used.

-**Share** at our comfort level. No one is asked to sing, pray or read aloud.

-**Are facilitated** by a leader who guides group discussion and pace.

Where to meet

Churches are convenient because they have kitchens, tables and are free, but also look for non-church, friendly alternatives like hotel conference or community rooms, homes, colleges, offices, and cafés.

Size Options: How large is your group? *(See also page 146.)*

One-on-One Get-Togethers	or	Small Group Meetings	or	Small/Large (8+) Group Gatherings

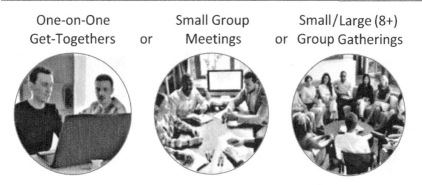

Time Options: How much time do you have?

Longer: WATCH > DISCOVER > RELATE with food as set out in this guide takes *2½ to 3 hours*. **This format is most impactful and cited below.** *

Medium: If limited to *1½ to 2 hours*, you will need to skip questions or just **read the first Discover section** to condense and keep up the pace.

Shorter: If the group has less time, say *an hour*, you could: 1) watch the episode and, 2) study the passages before coming. Then as you meet, you would discuss what you watched/studied in preparation. (This option is less than ideal if members' preparation is inconsistent.)

Note: All studies have a WATCH section. Studies #1, #4, #6, #7, #8 and #9 include two passages with TWO DISCOVER sections. If you are short on time, you could ask the group to study the first passage on their own and then study the second passage together.

#2, #3, #5, and #10 have one WATCH and one DISCOVER section: WATCH > DISCOVER > RELATE. Always plan on pacing yourselves to leave adequate time for the RELATE section at end of each study.

*EXAMPLE: Midweek Evening	***EXAMPLE: Saturday Morning**
5:45 ARRIVE: 15 min. to gather	**8:45 ARRIVE:** 15 min. to gather
6:00 POTLUCK: 30 min. to relax/eat	**9:00 LITE BREAKFAST:** 15 min.
6:30-8:45 *THE CHOSEN STUDY*	**9:15-11:30** *THE CHOSEN STUDY*

Guide Overview

The Chosen Study Guide provides a means of bringing people together to study and discuss Chosen episodes with Scripture. This framework gives direction to a wide variety of group studies and discussions:

How to Lead the Study

Tips to help current (and future) leaders prepare. Please read pages 18-19 thoroughly.

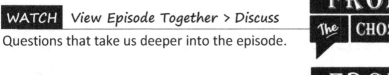

WATCH *View Episode Together > Discuss*

Questions that take us deeper into the episode.

DISCOVER *Read Text > Mark Up > Discuss*

Intro/"Look Fors"/Questions for passage's meaning.

RELATE *Apply Insights to God / Life / You > Discuss*

Personal questions that help us apply the passage to our lives.

Next two sections are for reference, not to discuss, unless time allows.*

NOTES on the Study **Commentary and Historical Context*

The biblical passages' context and meaning put into perspective.

*That's plausible but did it happen?

The Chosen's artistic license put into perspective.

HOME REFLECTION *Journaling, Commitments and Prayer*

Personal questions, ending with **Video Insights** and **T-Shirt Design**!

Don't use this as a Study Guide, but as a SCRATCH PAD!

What do you think about when you hear the word "study"? Yeah, thought so. It's bad. Well, how about when you hear the term, "Mark It Up"? Not so bad, right?

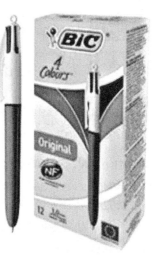

Think of a Mark-It-Up study format as the *adult version of drawing with crayons.*

When young children use crayons, they don't care about much except enjoying the process. That's the idea! Be like a kid. (We'll talk about this more in Study #4!) Just swap crayons for a four-color BIC pen!

We learn through our five senses, like hearing something read aloud. So, plan on having someone who reads well read the passages.

In marking up the Scripture passage, we also use another sense that we would otherwise not; the *sense of touch.* And if we do so colorfully (enter the four-color BIC pen—very inexpensive in a 12-pack from Amazon), we add just a bit more to the learning process through the *sense of sight.* **(For more in-depth info on *mark-it-up study*: page 159.)**

And don't worry about "drawing within the lines" or "color coding." Even if you tried, you just can't mess up this format. There's no right and wrong, there's just engagement. Hands on...literally.

So, think of this guide as a
SCRATCH PAD.
Apply the M-I-U format and have fun with it.
Yes, exactly like you did drawing those
childhood masterpieces!

Study and Discussion Format: WATCH > DISCOVER > RELATE

WATCH _View Episode 1 Together_ (54 min.) > _Discuss_

Example from Study #2, Episode One:
I Have Called You by Name

On next page

DISCOVER _Read Text > Mark It Up > Discuss_

Example from Study #2, Jesus, Simon, the Woman: Lk. 7:36-50

Ask the "W" Questions

WHO is involved | **WHEN** did it happen | **WHERE** is it happening |
WHAT is taking place | **HOW** is it happening... and then ask...
WHY questions to uncover the author's original meaning.

*The **"Look For"** at the end of each **INTRO** provides initial direction.

Mark Up the passage(s) by using a four-colored BIC pen to draw:

–Shapes around people or places.

–Boxes around whatever you'd like.

–Lines under key words and phrases.

–Clouds wherever you'd feel like it.

–Identify change of scene, watch for contrast, repetition, key words.

–Write notes.

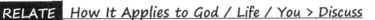
On next page

RELATE _How It Applies to God / Life / You > Discuss_

Express Your Thoughts:
Write / discuss / live out applications from the passages in your life— your relationship with God, with others, your values, priorities, goals.

How to WATCH The Chosen

Look up thechosen.tv under the "Watch" tab. For the app go
to thechosen.tv/app or search *The Chosen* in your Apple or
Android app store. From the app, you can stream to your TV.
You can find *The Chosen* on providers, like Amazon Prime too.

The
Chosen

Always ***turn on*** the *TV's closed captions* to better follow the narrative.
Darken *the room* to better follow the action. A big TV also helps!

Note: We identify the length of
each episode (from 19 to 53
minutes, excluding credits) in the
WATCH sections to help you pace
the study. Better to leave things
unsaid than to bog down.

How to DISCOVER *a passage's meaning*

Example from LUKE 7: ³⁶ One of Pharisees asked Jesus to eat with him,
To check Jesus out
and he went into the Pharisee's house and took his place at the
table. ³⁷And behold, a woman of the city, who was a sinner, when   she
Uninvited & Compelled
learned that he was reclining at table in the Pharisee's house, brought
an alabaster flask of ointment, ³⁸and standing behind him at his feet,
weeping, she began to wet his feet with her tears and wiped them with
Note the action words   *Inappropriate in public*
the hair of her head and kissed his feet and anointed them with
ointment. ³⁹Now when the Pharisee who had invited him saw this, he
said to himself, "If this man was a prophet, he would have known who
"sort" of woman   *Inappropriate to Simon*
and what sort of woman this is who is touching him, for she is a
sinner." ⁴⁰And Jesus answering said to him, "Simon, I have something
to say to you." And he answered, "Say it, Teacher."
Very deliberate personal address

How to use the guide's questions

Unlike most Bible studies, these studies take into account the fact that your group has just spent time studying (*Discover*). So, instead of using the guide's specific questions first, **start with "general questions,"** like:

... Set the scene, who's involved, and what are they doing?

... What did you see (observe/notice/appreciate) in this section?

... What strikes you (surprises you/is something new to you) here?

Then, ask general follow-up questions like: ... *Any other thoughts?*

Such questions often lead to an extended back-and-forth dialogue (see page 150). That's your discussion goal. If this happens, **you do not need to use many or any of the guide's more specific questions.** So, if/when the dialogue wanes or wanders from the main points, then you can use some of the guide's **more "specific questions,"** such as:

What does Jesus say are the results for those who are "born again"?

Contrast Jesus' attitude toward sinners with that of the Pharisees.

Home Reflection

The end of each study provides an occasion to meditate, journal and pray over important insights. We suggest that you find a special place and a special time to schedule this as a "God-encounter thing."

Such a time allows you to express praise, embrace gratitude, plan kindnesses, and evaluate where you are giving your time, energy, and focus: *Is this what God has for you—or is there something different?*

Note the wide variety of video resources here based on themes coming out of *The Chosen*. You can access these videos by typing in their URL or at thechosenstudy.org, under *Guides & Extras—Season One*.

Summarize each study in a T-Shirt Design!

The Chosen is big on merch—and so are we, except ours is drawn with a four-color BIC pen on a paper image. So, boil down your study's slogan or pick your favorite line from the episode—that's for the left-brained among us. For the right-brained, call on  the artist inside to draw your idea. And, yes, share it with your group!

One more idea for your home reflection

The Chosen: 40 Days with Jesus. *The Chosen* produces devotionals for each season. They are quite good. (See page 158 for more info.)

Longer options for Study #10 (See also page 118.)

Why should you consider a longer gathering for your last meeting?
and
Why bring up the last gathering even before you've had your first one?

Good questions. The answer requires a *big picture explanation*, so here goes: *The Chosen Study* is not meant to be a "normal Bible Study group." There certainly is nothing wrong with such studies. They're great, but they are just not what we're doing here. (For more, see pages 143-144.)

Our purpose centers around inviting everyone we know to join us for a study of Jesus and his message. In doing so, we seek to build enduring friendships between us, and that's how adding a day-long or weekend bonding event (at a special place!) can help us reach these goals.

Hopefully, your last gathering won't be your last meeting, but a key bonding opportunity to add fuel to the fire of momentum... for your next Chosen Study and the new group members who will join you!

For more input on how to create such longer events, see *Leaders* at thechosenstudy.org. On the next page are two basic options:

OPTION ONE: Day-Long Study #10 Event

9:00 Breakfast	**1:30** Review: Studies #1-5/Video clips
9:30 Study #10, pp. 118-132	**3:00** Review: Studies #6-10/Video clips
12:00 Lunch	**5:00** Dinner

OPTION TWO: Weekend Study #10 Retreat

FRIDAY: Dinner	**1:30** Afternoon session
7:00 Study #10, pp. 118-132	**6:00** Saturday Dinner
SATURDAY: Breakfast	**7:30** Evening Session
9:00 Morning session	**SUNDAY:** Breakfast
12:00 Saturday Lunch	**9:00** Morning session/End with Lunch

Leader's Notes: (See also pages 143-151.)

As you look back on the format, what do you find important or helpful?

–

–

–

–

–

Leaders: For helpful video explanations of *How to Lead a Chosen Study*, see tinyurl.com/how-to-lead and tinyurl.com/lead-and-promote.

We often use "tinyurl.com" to shorten the URL that would otherwise be required to type into your browser window to access a video.

A Word as We Begin

The Chosen is meant to take you into the eyes and ears of the people who followed Jesus. We believe that if you can see Jesus through the eyes of those who met him, you can be changed and impacted in the same way they were. If we can connect you with their burdens and struggles and questions, then ideally, we can connect you to the solution, to the answer to those questions.   –Dallas Jenkins

---

The Chosen Study supports these aspirations by pairing *The Chosen* with Old and New Testament passages to take us deeper—together!
                                                    –The Chosen Study Team

---

Starting a Chosen Study? Let us know: thechosenstudy.org/join and connect with others doing so: facebook.com/thechosenstudy. Thanks!

 **PRIOR to STUDY**

Leading Season One—preparation checklist

Leader's Note: *Buy guides and four-colored BIC pens in advance.* Participants can purchase guides themselves but it's often easier if one person buys the guides (from Amazon or other bookstores) along with four-color BIC pens (find 6/12 BIC pen packs on Amazon). We keep the guides affordable to encourage their widespread use. To see all our guides and to order—including **volume discounts**(!)—see: thechosenstudy.com/order.

Buy some extra guides for new people and those who forget to bring theirs—it will happen. **Label these as *EXTRA* on the back cover** to use for others in subsequent weeks. Feel free to charge the participants a small fee for reimbursement of these purchases.

If someone forgets their guide and there are no extras, go to the website **to get the PDF by typing in URL:** thechosenstudy.org/season-one

−*Study the passage(s) and take notes on the episodes* ahead of time. Look at the *Notes* after the questions (and other commentaries, as you see fit), as well as the *Real But Realistic?* sections.

−*Spend time preparing using Prior To Study* on page 19, etc. Mark It Up! **Page 19 is the template. All other studies follow a similar pattern.**

Always tell your group at which question to end, so they know how far to go during the study/discussion time.

Keep up the pace! You often think you have more time than you do, so closely monitor time, leave things unsaid, and keep moving to end on time. (Ask your group for permission to interrupt to keep up the pace!)

NOTE TO EVERYONE: *Chosen Study guides* are not meant to be static presentations. We are open to your review, comments, and edits. If you find helpful, related videos, or commentary presentations, please let us know at thechosenstudy.org/join.

Leading Study #1—facilitating checklist

-Begin by exchanging names and personal info. Put together a sign-up sheet. (See page 152-153 and sign-up sheet on website under *Resources*.)

-Have members put their names on the back cover for identification.

-Identify your time constraints and group size. (See pages 9 and 146.)

-Go through the Eight Ground Rules on page 147. Talk about signing **the Page 147 Challenge** of consistent attendance. We're not here to lay on guilt, but consistency serves everyone. Have fun with stressing this!

-Discuss the format by *walking through* pages 10 to 15 with the group.

-Read or summarize the Intro and the "Look For" on page 22 and have a prepared volunteer read aloud the passages (pages 22-24).

-Give members some time for personal study on passages using their four-color BIC pens. Monitor to end study time when appropriate.

-Discuss first four passages by asking general discussion questions, then specific ones in small/large group as time allows (see page 14).

-Watch the episode and discuss (page 24).

-Have a prepped volunteer read the Intro and passage (pages 25-26).

-Give members some time for personal study using BIC pens. Monitor group(s) to end study time when appropriate. **Keep up the pace!**

-Discuss the passage by asking general, then specific questions (p. 14).

-Spend time in reflection/writing and discuss the Relate questions. Point out the Home Reflection, Video Insights and T-Shirt sections (page 29-31). For links to the videos, see thechosenstudy/season-one.

Notes: What are the important things for you to focus on?

-

-

-

-

-

-

-

-

-

-

-

-

The Shepherd   Study #1

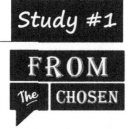

BACKGROUND: From the beginning, *The Chosen* has been unusual. Born out of the seeds of a Hollywood box office flop, the creator, Dallas Jenkins, wondered if he had what it took to ever make an appealing movie.

Dallas's church asked him to create a short film for Christmas (aka, *The Shepherd,* now the Pilot episode), and from this film he and the Angel Studios team went on to initiate the largest crowdfunded media production in history—to the tune of over 10 million dollars given by 75,346 enthusiastic fans: Season One of *The Chosen.*

The plan continued: Have each season crowdfund the next one until they complete all seven seasons. The series is free and funded by people interested in "paying it forward." And now it's time to watch it, study it, discuss it, and live it forward.

NOTE TO EVERYONE: To hear Dallas talk about the story behind *The Chosen,* see: tinyurl.com/the-chosen-story. It's well worth it.

DISCOVER *Read Aloud > Mark It Up > Discuss*

INTRO: Old Testament prophets anticipated the coming Messiah. In Study #1's pilot episode, we are introduced to two such prophets quoted in four different texts. But there's a problem: *Were the Jewish leaders looking for the right Messiah?* (For historical background on these prophecies, see the Notes on pages 28-29.) ***Start wtih using your pen to underline the words describing the one coming.***

The Ruler to Be Born in Bethlehem
MICAH 5 ² But you, O Bethlehem Ephrathah,

> who are too little to be among the clans of Judah,

> from you shall come forth for me

> one who is to be ruler in Israel,

> whose coming forth is from of old,

> from ancient days.

> ³ Therefore he shall give them up until the time

> when she who is in labor has given birth;

> then the rest of his brothers shall return to the people

> of Israel.... ⁵ And he shall be their peace.

For to Us a Child Is Born
ISAIAH 9 ² The people walking in darkness

> have seen a great light;

> on those living in the land of deep darkness

> a light has dawned.

> ³ You have enlarged the nation

> and increased their joy;

> they rejoice before you

as people rejoice at the harvest,

as warriors rejoice

when dividing the plunder.

⁴ For as in the day of Midian's defeat,

you have shattered

the yoke that burdens them,

the bar across their shoulders,

the rod of their oppressor.

⁵ Every warrior's boot used in battle

and every garment rolled in blood

will be destined for burning,

will be fuel for the fire.

⁶ For to us a child is born,

to us a son is given,

and the government will be on his shoulders.

And he will be called

Wonderful Counselor, Mighty God,

Everlasting Father, Prince of Peace.

⁷ Of the greatness of his government and peace

there will be no end.

He will reign on David's throne

and over his kingdom,

establishing and upholding it

with justice and righteousness

from that time on and forever.

The zeal of the LORD Almighty

will accomplish this.

The Ransomed Shall Return

ISAIAH 35 ³ Strengthen the weak hands,

and make firm the feeble knees.

⁴ Say to those who have an anxious heart,

"Be strong; fear not!

Behold, your God

will come with vengeance,

with the recompense of God.

He will come and save you."

⁵ Then the eyes of the blind shall be opened,

and the ears of the deaf unstopped;

⁶ then shall the lame man leap like a deer,

and the tongue of the mute sing for joy.

For waters break forth in the wilderness,

and streams in the desert

The Sign of Immanuel

ISAIAH 7 ¹⁴ Therefore the Lord himself will give you a sign.

Behold, the virgin shall conceive and bear a son,

and shall call his name Immanuel.

1. *How do these prophets describe the Messiah and his coming?*

WATCH View Pilot Episode under Bonus Content: The short film
that inspired **The Chosen** (19 min., from 0:30 to 19:23)
or on YouTube (search: The Chosen: The Shepherd) > **Discuss**

INTRO: *The Shepherd* (pilot episode) asks and, to
some degree, answers what kind of Messiah the
Jewish nation and the world should expect.

2. *From the film, how would you describe the shepherd's encounter:*
... with the religious leaders?

... with Joseph and Mary?

... with the angelic hosts?

... with the baby Jesus?

DISCOVER Read Aloud > Mark It Up > Discuss

INTRO: The affairs of state get interrupted by the
affairs of heaven in a Bethlehem manger. An
unprepared world receives a unique baby boy. *Use
the "W" questions (page 12) to see what's there.*

The Birth of Jesus Christ

LUKE 2 In those days a decree went out from Caesar Augustus that all the world should be registered. [2] This was the first registration when Quirinius was governor of Syria. [3] And all went to be registered, each to his own town.

[4] And Joseph also went up from Galilee, from the town of Nazareth to Judea, to the city of David, which is called Bethlehem, because he was of the house and lineage of David, [5] to be registered with Mary, his betrothed, who was with child. [6] While they were there, the time came for her to give birth. [7] And she gave birth to her firstborn son and wrapped him in swaddling cloths and laid him in a manger, because there was no place for them in the inn.

The Shepherds and the Angels

[8] And in the same region there were shepherds out in the field, keeping watch over their flock by night. [9] And an angel of the Lord appeared to them, and the glory of the Lord shone around them, and they were filled with great fear. [10] And the angel said to them, "Fear not, for behold, I bring you good news of great joy that will be for all the people. [11] For unto you is born this day in the city of David a Savior, who is Christ the Lord. [12] And this will be a sign for you: you will find a baby wrapped in swaddling cloths and lying in a manager." [13] And suddenly there was with the angel a multitude of the heavenly host praising God and saying, [14] "Glory to God in the highest, and on earth

peace among those with whom he is pleased!"

¹⁵ When the angels went away from them into heaven, the shepherds said to one another, "Let us go over to Bethlehem and see this thing that has happened, which the Lord has made known to us."

¹⁶ And they went with haste and found Mary and Joseph, and the baby lying in a manger. ¹⁷ And when they saw it, they made known the saying that had been told them concerning this child. ¹⁸ And all who heard it wondered at what the shepherds told them. ¹⁹ But Mary treasured up all these things, pondering them in her heart. ²⁰ And the shepherds returned, glorifying and praising God for all they had heard and seen, as it had been told them.

²¹ And at the end of eight days, when he was circumcised, he was called Jesus, the name given by the angel before he was conceived in the womb.

3. There are both *ordinary* and *cosmic* elements to the story of Jesus' birth. *What stands out to you about his birth?*

4. Bethlehem is about six miles south of Jerusalem and 80-90 miles from Nazareth (see map on pages 138-139). *What do you imagine that Joseph's and Mary's journey and accommodations were like?*

5. *How does the story of Jesus' birth help us understand the nature and role of the Messiah?*

RELATE *How It Applies to God / Life / You > Discuss*

6. Let's say you had never heard the story of Jesus' birth. *What would appeal to you, surprise you, or even make you uncomfortable?*

NOTES on Study #1 *Commentary and Historical Context*

Micah 5:2-5—The Ruler to Be Born in Bethlehem Ephrathah

- There is a southern Bethlehem (Ephrathah) and a northern Bethlehem. Micah proclaimed his messages against spiritual decay in Samaria and Jerusalem during the reigns of Jotham (742-735 BC), Ahaz (735-715 BC) and Hezekiah (715-686 BC). The Assyrians conquered Israel's northern ten tribes in 721 BC and deported many of her citizens. In the face of great failure, Micah raises the hope of God's salvation, embodied in a coming ruler to be born in a small backwater village.

Isaiah 9:2-7—For to Us a Child Is Born

- As the northern kingdom was about to be attacked and taken into captivity, the southern kingdom, under King Ahaz, entered a time of increasing distress and darkness as a vassal state of Assyria (eventually conquered by Babylon in 586 BC). With national collapse on the horizon, Isaiah proclaimed the coming of the Messiah to lead his people to victory and to bring an era of light, joy, and peace.

- Who would be the one to overthrow these oppressors and banish war? Shockingly, God will raise up a child—a newborn, no less—to deliver his people and establish justice. This child is not part of an earthly government, but he carries with him a heavenly one.

Isaiah 35:3-6—The Ransomed Shall Return

- Jesus begins his ministry in his hometown of Nazareth by claiming the power that Isaiah prophesied 700 years earlier would attend the

Messiah's coming. (Compare Isaiah 35:3-6, pages 23, and Isaiah 61:1-2, with Luke 4:18-19 on page 58.)

- Jesus makes his Messianic legitimacy clear to John the Baptist who, in prison, wondered if Jesus really was the Messiah. When John's disciples put this question to Jesus, he answered them, *Go and tell John what you hear and see: the blind receive their sight, and the lame walk, and lepers are cleansed, and the deaf hear, and the dead are raised up, and the poor have good news preached to them. And blessed is the one who is not offended by me* (Matthew 11:4-6).

Isaiah 7:14—The Sign of Immanuel
- The promised child is virgin-born, named *Immanuel*: God with us!

Luke 2:1-21—The Birth of Jesus Christ
- Jesus' story is unlike Greek mythology. It is rooted in history during the noteworthy reign of Caesar Augustus (31 BC – 14 AD), the great-nephew of Julius Caesar. After eventually besting his rivals, Augustus brought about a peaceful and thriving rule, the *Pax Romana*.

- "When Quirinus was governor of Syria" (2:2) is another historical anchor. Joseph and Mary travel nearly 90 miles from Nazareth to their ancestral home, Bethlehem, to register for a census. Luke tells the story of ordinary people caught up in a grand, cosmic event.

 *That's plausible but did it happen?*

Was there a once lame shepherd who first saw Jesus? We have no such reference. One would not be surprised, however, if the Messiah's arrival could have had made such an impact on those who encountered him (Isaiah 35:3-6; compare Matthew 11:4-6; Luke 4:18-19).

Did that shepherd share water with Mary before the birth of Jesus?
We don't know. Joseph and Mary were likely expecting to stay with relatives or in an inn after their long trip. Once there, they found no place for the birth except a stable. A small act of kindness, however, fits the theme of God providing water for the thirsty, and foreshadows a theme developed in Episode 8, with a role reversal of sorts.

HOME REFLECTION *Journaling, Commitments and Prayer*

7. The word "audacious" means surprisingly bold, risky, imprudent, even lacking respect. *In what way was Jesus' birth audacious?*

8. *How does Jesus' birth story make him more appealing to you?*

The Chosen: **40 Days with Jesus.** *The Chosen* produces a devotional for each season which can be used five days a week over the course of the study. We highly recommend it. (See page 158 for more info.)

Video Insights: What is the Gospel? –Melissa Dougherty
Type in URL: tinyurl.com/the-gospel-defined (20:24 min.)
(Type URL precisely in your browser on device or go to website under *Guides*.)

Notes: Other Videos:

After watching > discovering > relating,
what slogan would you write or draw on your T-shirt?

Draft concepts:

Final design:

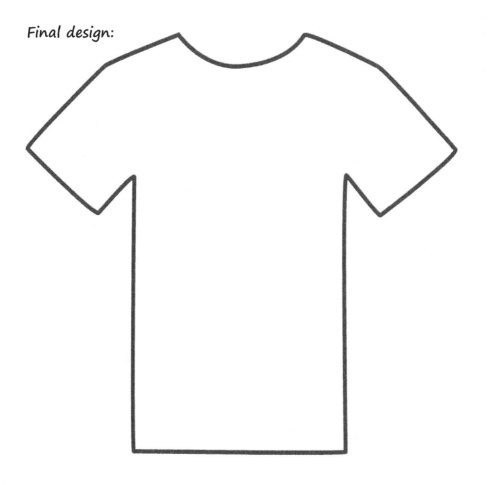

 **Getting ready for the next study.**

–Begin with new people introducing themselves and again point out the ground rules on page 147.

–*Briefly reacquaint your group with the study format* on pages 12-13, especially the "W" questions and using the BIC pens. *At the end of all the DISCOVER INTROs is a clue of what to "Look For" in the passage.*

NOTE TO EVERYONE: *HOME REFLECTION.* The Chosen Study is not written with the expectation that participants do prior preparation. However, we do encourage a post-study time of reflection (as on pages 29-31 and 39-41) to journal, consider life-commitments, and to pray.

So, schedule time, maybe as part of a weekly Sabbath (we'll talk about this in Study #3), to go deeper with the content's application in your life. Oh, and do feel free to look/study ahead of time if you'd like!

You've also likely noted a suggested video for *further insight* (pages 30, 40, etc.). These videos are meant to introduce you to those who are speaking about *The Chosen* or on its themes and take you deeper into the content. To access, it is necessary to **precisely type into the URL** in your computer, device or phone's browser window for the YouTube videos.

Speaking of going deeper, Dallas interviews an Evangelical, Messianic Jew, and Catholic scholar for each episode of Season One. You can access those interviews, here: tinyurl.com/deep-dives.

Finally, you can more directly access these videos from our website, thechosenstudy.org, under *Guides & Extras—Season One.*

I Have Called You by Name

INTRO: We begin in 2 BC with **Mary Magdalene** as a little girl being comforted by her father. The episode then transitions to 28 AD, 30 years later. Mary is possessed by seven demons (Luke 8:2), and in such distress that her name (in *The Chosen*) had been changed to Lilith, a name that means "night monster" (see page 39).

Along the way, we meet several characters that develop the storylines further: **Quintus**, the Roman Praetor of Galilee; **Nicodemus**, a Jewish Pharisee, both concerned about Jews fishing on *Shabbat* (the Sabbath) but for different reasons; Nicodemus' wife, **Zohara**; **Matthew**, a despised Jewish tax collector; his Roman centurion escort, **Gaius**; the fishermen brothers, **Andrew** and **Simon**; plus, Simon's wife, **Eden**.

WATCH **View Episode 1** (52 min. from 0:00 to 52:14) > **Discuss**

1. *From the film's depiction, what stood out to you about each person, their situation, and dilemma:*

... *Simon and Andrew?*

... *Matthew?*

... *Nicodemus?*

2. *How would you characterize Mary's situation when we first meet her as a young girl? And now, 30 years later?*

3. Note the Scripture that Mary's father used to comfort her as a girl, and that Jesus speaks to her (leaving off "O Jacob" and O Israel"):

"Thus says the Lord, he who created you, O Jacob, he who formed you, O Israel: Fear not, for I have redeemed you; I have called you by name, you are mine" (Isaiah 43:1}.

What struck you about Mary's encounter with Jesus in the tavern and his quoting of Isaiah 43:1 to her?

DISCOVER Read Aloud > Mark It Up > Discuss

INTRO: Mary Magdalene is from Magdala, a fishing town on the western shore of the Sea of Galilee. She is referenced twelve times in the New Testament. In Luke 8:2-3, the author lists her as one of the women who traveled with Jesus and helped support him.

That same passage says that seven demons were driven out of her. Mary ends up being a witness to the Crucifixion, the empty tomb and the first to see the risen Christ. Possibly, she is the woman described in this passage. Whether it is really her or not, this story describes well the kind of person Mary Magdalene becomes. ***Look especially for the contrasts between characters in this passage.***

Jesus' Message: A Debt, Forgiveness and Love

LUKE 7: [36] One of the Pharisees asked Jesus to eat with him, and he went into the Pharisee's house and took his place at the table. [37] And behold, a woman of the city, who was a sinner, when she learned that he was reclining at table in the Pharisee's house, brought an alabaster flask of ointment, [38] and standing behind him at his feet, weeping, she began to wet his feet with her tears and wiped them with the hair of her head and kissed his feet and anointed them with the ointment.

[39]Now when the Pharisee who had invited him saw this, he said to himself, "If this man was a prophet, he would have known who and what sort of woman this is who is touching him, for she is a sinner."

[40]And Jesus answering said to him, "Simon, I have something to say to you. "And he answered, "Say it, Teacher." [41] "A certain moneylender had two debtors. One owed five hundred denarii, and the other fifty. [42] When they could not pay, he cancelled the debt of both. Now which

of them will love him more?"

43 Simon answered, "The one, I suppose, for whom he cancelled the larger debt."

And he said to him, "You have judged rightly."

44 Then turning toward the woman he said to Simon, "Do you see this woman? I entered your house; you gave me no water for my feet, but she has wet my feet with her tears and wiped them with her hair. 45 You gave me no kiss, but from the time I came in she has not ceased to kiss my feet. 46 You did not anoint my head with oil, but she has anointed my feet with ointment. 47 Therefore I tell you, her sins, which are many, are forgiven—for she loved much. But he who is forgiven little, loves little."

48 And he said to her, "Your sins are forgiven."

49 Then those who were at table with him began to say among themselves, "Who is this, who even forgives sins?"

50 And he said to the woman, "Your faith has saved you; go in peace."

4. *What stood out to you about this dinner party?*

5. *How would you contrast Simon (the Pharisee) with the woman?*

6. A 500 denarii debt equals two years of salary and a 50 denarii debt, two months' salary. *What does this parable illustrate about the two debtors?*

7. Jesus contrasts Simon's and the woman's actions toward him. *How do their responses show their understanding of their debt, the forgiveness offered, and the response made?* Use the chart if helpful.

	Simon	Woman
Amount of Debt (Recognized)?		
Forgiveness Offered/Received?		
Response Made?		

8. *Why is Simon unable to recognize that he is a debtor?*

9. *What was Jesus' message to Simon?*

... his message to the woman?

RELATE How It Applies to God / Life / You > Discuss

10. *How would, or does, a recognition of being forgiven affect your view of others and of God?*

NOTES on Study #2 *Commentary and Historical Context*

Luke 7:36-50—Jesus' Message: A Debt, Forgiveness and Love

- The issue of being religious but unloving (Simon) versus being non-religious—"a sinner"—but loving (the woman), challenges us. With whom do we identify most? Do we come to God on our own terms, in self-righteous pride—or on his terms, in humility?

- What Simon didn't do was considered a customary greeting when an honored guest arrived at one's home.

- The issue that love is a result of experiencing forgiveness, not the other way around, is seen in the woman's motivation. When it comes to God, we don't start by loving, we start by being loved.

- The gospel message is well-portrayed in the story and in the parable: (1) We all have an *unpayable debt* (as sinners); (2) *debt is canceled* (through forgiveness); resulting in, (3) a *transformed response* (love).

 That's plausible but did it happen?

Was Simon married? Yes, as he had a mother-in-law (Mark 129-31), but we don't know his wife's name or any specifics about her.

Did Matthew collect taxes from fishermen like Simon and Andrew?
We do not know from Scripture, but it's likely. Matthew was a tax collector operating around the Sea of Galilee (Mark 2:13-14). His concern about these two particular fishermen being able to "square their account" would have been an ongoing concern for any Jewish business under the heavy hand of Roman taxation.

Did Nicodemus travel to Galilee to teach students?
Maybe, but he met Jesus in Jerusalem, not Capernaum (John 2:29–3:1).

Did Nicodemus try to heal Mary Magdalene?
Mary was delivered from seven demons (Luke 8:1-2), but there is no record of Nicodemus ever meeting her, nor where it took place.

Is Zohara, the wife of Nicodemus, in the gospel record?
She is not mentioned, but her character in *The Chosen* helps to demonstrate the divergence of opinions about Jesus, which are beginning to surface between Nicodemus and others in his circle.

Is there significance in Mary's name, *Lilith*, when possessed?
Yes, Lilith was a demonic figure in Jewish folklore whose name was thought to derive from a class of Mesopotamian demons and meant "night monster" with a cult following that lasted to the 7th Century. But we do not know what her demon-possessed name was or even if she had one. Regardless, Mary is completely cleansed of their influence.

HOME REFLECTION *Journaling, Commitments and Prayer*

11. *On the following continuum, put an "X" on the line in the place that best describes your relationship with God/Jesus right now.*

Observer...   Skeptic...   Learner...   Seeker...   Follower...

12. *Do you want to move further to the right on the spectrum as shown on the previous page? If so, what might that mean for you?*

13. *Who could help, and what could you do to encourage such growth?*

Video Insights: Good News from Luke 7:36–50 –Bill Syrios

Type in URL: tinyurl.com/good-news-from-Luke7 (24:33 min)

Notes: **Other Videos:**

After watching > discovering > relating,
what slogan would you write or draw on your T-shirt?

Draft concepts:

Final design:

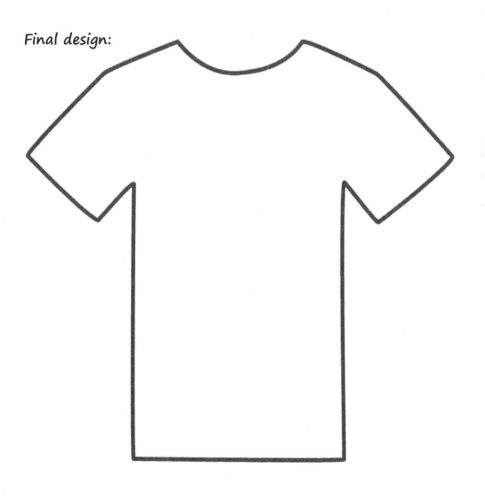

Shabbat Reading

This reading is recited before partaking of the *Shabbat* (Sabbath) meal, exalting God's creation and Israel's blessing.

Now the heavens and the earth were completed, and all their hosts, and God completed on the seventh day all His work that He did. And God abstained on the seventh day from all the work He did. And God blessed the seventh day, and He hallowed it, for thereon He abstained from all the work that God created to do. Blessed are you, Lord our God, Ruler of the universe, who created the fruit of the vine. You have lovingly and willingly given us your Shabbat as an inheritance in memory of creation. Because this is the first day of our holy assemblies in memory of the Exodus from Egypt. Blessed are you, Lord our God, King of the universe, who brings forth the bread from the earth. Amen

Eshet Chayil
Ode to Women of Valor
that also exalts the rhythm of work and rest.

Proverbs 31:10-31 is, likewise, recited or sung before the Shabbat meal as praise to women, and a blessing to children. *Valor can be defined as a great force of courage.* The Ode begins as follows:

A woman of valor, who can find?
Her worth is far beyond that of jewels....

NOTE TO EVERYONE: This study includes a video from the *Bible Project* called *Sabbath*. You can find their extensive video collections on books of the Bible, biblical themes, word studies, and sketched-out videos for every book in the Bible and more at <u>bibleproject.com</u>. (See page 139.)

Shabbat

Study #3

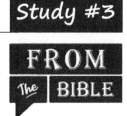

INTRO: *Shabbat* (aka "the Sabbath") was given to Israel 4,000 years ago as a practice that celebrates God "resting" on the seventh day from the work of Creation. This example acts as a weekly reminder for his people to slow down, reassess, and focus on what is most important: our family, our friends, our calling, and God himself.

Let's slow down ourselves to look at God's six days of work in creation and the seventh day pattern of rest that he set for those he made in his image.

Use one color to underline what is the same each day; with another color highlight what is different each day. (Or circle, box, or cloud it!)

DISCOVER Read Aloud > Mark It Up > Discuss

The Creation of the World (. . . a condensed version)
GENESIS 1 In the beginning, God created the heavens and the earth. [2] The earth was without form and void, and darkness was over the face of the deep. And the Spirit of God was hovering over the face of the waters.

[3] And God said, "Let there be light," and there was light. [4] And God saw that the light was good. And God separated the light from the darkness. [5] God called the light Day, and the darkness he called Night. And there was evening and there was morning, **the first day**.

[6] And God said, "Let there be an expanse in the midst of the waters, and let it separate the waters from the waters." . . . [8] And God called the expanse Heaven. And there was evening and there was morning, **the second day**. . . . [10] And God saw that it was good.

[11] And God said, "Let the earth sprout vegetation, plants yielding seed, and fruit trees bearing fruit in which is their seed, each according to its kind, on the earth." . . . [12] And God saw that it was good. [13] And there was evening and there was morning, **the third day**.

[14] And God said, "Let there be lights in the expanse of the heavens to separate the day from the night. And let them be for signs and for seasons, and for days and years. . . . [18] And God saw that it was good. [19] And there was evening and there was morning, **the fourth day.**

[20] And God said, "Let the waters swarm with swarms of living creatures, and let birds fly above the earth across the expanse of the heavens." . . . [21] And God saw that it was good. [22] And God blessed them, saying, "Be fruitful and multiply and fill the waters in the seas. . . ." [23] And there was evening and there was morning, **the fifth day**.

[24] And God said, "Let the earth bring forth living creatures according to their kinds." . . . [25] And God saw that it was good.

[26] Then God said, "Let us make man in our image, after our likeness. And let them have dominion over the fish of the sea and over the birds of the heavens and over the livestock and over all the earth and over every creeping thing that creeps on the earth."

[27] So God created man in his own image, in the image of God
he created him; male and female he created them.

[28] And God blessed them. And God said to them, "Be fruitful and multiply and fill the earth and subdue it," . . . [31] And God saw everything that he had made, and behold, it was very good. And there was evening and there was morning, **the sixth day**.

The Seventh Day, God Rested

GENESIS 2 Thus the heavens and the earth were finished, and all the host of them. [2] And on **the seventh day** God finished his work that he had done, and he rested on the seventh day from all his work that he had done. [3] **So God blessed the seventh day and made it holy, because on it God rested from all his work that he had done in creation.**

Remember the Sabbath

EXODUS 20 [8] "Remember the Sabbath day, to keep it holy. [9] Six days you shall labor, and do all your work, [10] but **the seventh day** is a Sabbath to the Lord your God. On it you shall not do any work, you, or your son, or your daughter, your male servant, or your female servant, or your livestock, or the sojourner who is within your gates. [11] **For in six days the Lord made heaven and earth, the sea, and all that is in them, and rested on the seventh day. Therefore, the Lord blessed the Sabbath day and made it holy.**

1. "In the beginning": The first thing God created was time. He then set aside six days (or periods of time) to fashion creation.
   What stands out to you:
   ... about his process of creating our world?

   ... about the mention of his pleasure ("it was good") in the process?

   ... about the creation of humanity on Day Six?

2. *What do you learn about the origin and meaning of the Sabbath on Day Seven?*

3. The thought of God "resting" is rather unusual. *What do you think this reference implies?*

WATCH *View Episode 2* (38 min., from 1:25 to 39:17) > **Discuss**

INTRO: Nicodemus (*teacher of teachers*) is a member of the Sanhedrin, the Jewish high court that included 70 members. The **Av Beit Din** presided as its second highest-ranking member  and *The Chosen* includes him also visiting Capernaum. Nicodemus's students, **Shmuel** and **Yussif,** make more of an appearance, and we are introduced to Jesus' first two students, **"Little" James** and **Thaddeus.**

4. *What stood out to you about each of their situations or dilemmas as expressed in the four Shabbat meals:*

... for Matthew and his dog?

... for Simon, Eden (Simon's wife), and Andrew?

... for Nicodemus, Zohara, and company?

... for Mary, Jesus, and company?

5. *What did you think of how Mary describes her changed life to Nicodemus, and later, her introduction of Jesus to her guests as "the man who helped me?"*

WATCH BibleProject.com video: **Sabbath** (5 min.) > Discuss
(tinyurl.com/sabbath-bible-project)

6. *From this video, how would you describe the expanded meaning and purpose of the Sabbath?* (You may want to watch it again!)

RELATE How It Applies to God / Life / You > Discuss

7. How would Sabbath rest differ from sleep or being on vacation?

8. How might you make better use of the Sabbath as a weekly reset, including the reminder of God's presence and his work around us?

NOTES on Study #3 Commentary and Historical Context

Genesis 1:1-31—The Creation of the World

- The word for "day" in Hebrew is *yom*. This word's meaning is not precise and depends on its context. So, whether this period of Creation was six 24-hour days or six billion years, each increment is poetically celebrated as *good*...and finally *very good*.

Genesis 2:1-3—The Seventh Day, God Rested

- God honors his six days of work with a seventh day of rest, which he blessed and made "holy," (meaning *set apart*). How appropriate he rests right after creating humanity—uniquely made in his image and commended to help him manage his creative work!

Exodus 20:8-11—Remember the Sabbath

- It's hard to fathom what it means that the Creator of the Universe somehow paused to rest. As the meaning of the Sabbath becomes increasingly clear in Exodus 20:8-11 and beyond, his actions are more for us, his creatures, as a model for living well. **Question:** *If we can't work 1/7 of our potential amount of work time, how will we make it?* **Answer:** *By depending on God, that he will come through for us.*

That's plausible but did it happen?

Did the Jews save a seat for Elijah during the Passover? Yes, observant Jews do this during Passover (not every Sabbath) to honor the expectation that Elijah would come again to herald the Messiah (Malachi 4:5). Jesus indicates, however, that John the Baptist fulfilled this expectation of Elijah's ministry (Matthew 11:14).

Were the disciples as young as Matthew looks?
Quite likely Jesus' disciples were young—perhaps most were under age 18, some as young as 15. The reasons for this are deduced from Jewish tradition, historical context, and a few clues from Scripture. In Jesus' day, a Jewish man received a wife after age 18. Simon was the only one known to have been married. (In Matthew 8:14-15, it was his mother-in-law, named Dasha in this film, which Jesus healed.)

So, we may presume the others were young—either teens, too young to be married, or slightly older bachelors, but still young, without the family responsibilities Simon had.

The tradition of education, which formally ended at age 15 at that time, also indicates a youthful band of brothers. Higher education (for those wealthy or gifted enough) consisted of studying under a local rabbi who accepted some very young men as students; otherwise, they entered the workforce by their mid-teens, usually apprenticed under their fathers in the family business.

Was there an issue of Jews fishing on the Sabbath?
Unsure, but it's reasonable to assume so. Jews were under Roman occupation, so when it came to avoiding paying taxes, you can be assured that they searched for any possible way out, which for some, meant violating the Sabbath. Episode 4 will expand on this issue.

Did Simon betray the other fishermen?
There is no record that he had a *tax problem,* so there would have been no reason for him to consider betraying his fellow Jews.

NOTE TO EVERYONE: It is not an unfair development for *The Chosen* writers to give Simon a sense of desperation—having massive, unpaid taxes. And desperate times can call for desperate measures—wagering on fights or selling out fellow fishermen to the Romans. But, while this backstory makes for an intriguing and even plausible storyline, we have no biblical evidence that Simon had tax debts in the first place.

The potential problem stems from the powerful, visual nature of film (and the music score behind it) that can easily sweep us up and have us assigning meaning from it to the written word. We would say, do both: study what the Scripture actually says, and enjoy the captivating ride *The Chosen* takes us on—but learn the difference!

If you'd like more input on this, check out Dallas' videos, *Can you trust The Chosen?* and the *Interview of Jonathan Roumie*, the actor who portrays Jesus. See page 140 for more info and those video links.

| HOME REFLECTION | Journaling, Commitments and Prayer |

9. Set aside time (next Sabbath!?) to evaluate your schedule and your pace of life and ask: *How well am I living according to my priorities?*

10. *What changes will you consider making:*

   ...in your relationship with God?

... in the lives of key family members (spouse, children, etc.)?

... in how you are living your life or spending your time?

Video Insights: The Jewish Observation of Shabbat
Type in URL: tinyurl.com/the-shabbat –Rabbi Jason Sobel

Notes: **Other Videos:**   (9:03 min.)

After watching > discovering > relating, what slogan would you write or draw on your T-shirt?

Draft concepts:

Final design:

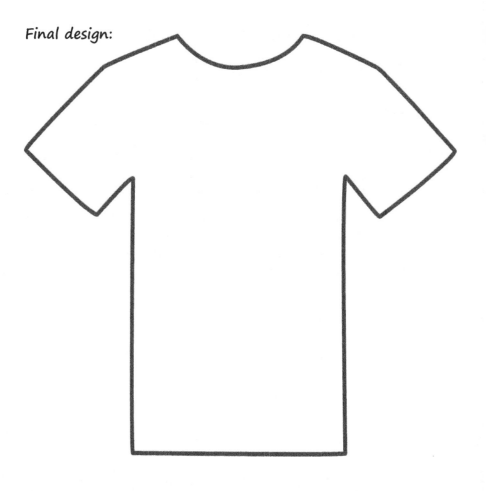

 **Some reminders**

Remember, always tell your group at which question to end, so they know how far to go during the study/discussion time.

Keep up the pace! You often think you have more time than you do, so, closely monitor your time, leave things unsaid, and keep moving to end on time.

NOTE FOR EVERYONE: *Inviting new people—is it too late?* No way! The beauty of *The Chosen Study* is that new members can come in at any time and binge watch to catch up! Additionally, we've seen people go through each Season multiple times.

Who to invite? Anyone who fits on this list: friends, loved ones, family members, colleagues, teammates, acquaintances, those who cross your path—if they're curious, if they're willing to check it—then come!

Jesus Loves the Little Children

Study #4

INTRO: Who doesn't love children? Well, the disciples seem to have serious issues with them. Granted, children can be inconvenient, but not so  to Jesus. Not only is he drawn to "the least of these," he also recognizes the power that childlike meekness and openness has as an object lesson for faith.

Use your pen to mark comparisons between a child and "whoever."

DISCOVER Read Aloud > Mark It Up > Discuss

Matthew 19: [13] Then children were brought to him that he might lay his hands on them and pray. The disciples rebuked the people, [14] but Jesus said, "Let the little children come to me and do not hinder them, for to such belongs the kingdom of heaven." [15] And he laid his hands on them.

Who Is the Greatest?
Matthew 18: The disciples asked Jesus, "Who is the greatest in the kingdom of heaven?"

[2] And calling to him a child, he put him in the midst of them [3] and said, "Truly, I say to you, unless you turn and become like children, you will never enter the kingdom of heaven. [4] Whoever humbles himself like this child is the greatest in the kingdom of heaven.

[5] "Whoever receives one such child in my name receives me, [6] but whoever causes one of these little ones who believe in me to sin, it would be better for him to have a great millstone fastened around his neck and to be drowned in the depth of the sea.

1. What is the difference between the disciples' approach and Jesus' approach with these children?

2. What about children make them good object lessons for faith?

3. Jesus calls his disciples to "turn" in verse 3. *What are they to turn from and turn toward?*

WATCH **View Episode 3** (*28 min., from 0:00 to 28:23*) > **Discuss**

INTRO: The irrepressible **Abigail**, and her friend, **Joshua** "the Brave," lead a group of children who spend the entire episode with Jesus. Losing their initial shyness, the group is put to work by Jesus,  and they find themselves becoming his youngest, most inquisitive students.

4. *What stood out to you about the questions the children ask Jesus?*

... about his response to them?

5. *How does he teach them in a playful and purposeful way?*

DISCOVER Read Aloud > Mark It Up > Discuss

INTRO: When pressed by Abigail, *what is your reason for being here?* Jesus tells the children what he told his hometown synagogue based on the words of Isaiah 61 (in vv. 18-19), but with a

different response. (See page 61 for some historical background.) ***Trace out the people's reactions to Jesus and how and why they change.***

Jesus Begins his Ministry

LUKE 4: [14] And Jesus returned in the power of the Spirit to Galilee, and a report about him went out through all the surrounding country.

[15] And he taught in their synagogues, being glorified by all.

[16] And he came to Nazareth, where he had been brought up. As was his

custom, he went to the synagogue on the Sabbath day, and he stood

up to read. [17] And the scroll of the prophet Isaiah was given to him. He

unrolled the scroll and found the place where it was written,

> [18] "The Spirit of the Lord is upon me,
>
>> because he has anointed me
>>
>> to proclaim good news to the poor.
>
> He has sent me to proclaim liberty to the captives
>
>> and recovering of sight to the blind,
>>
>> to set at liberty those who are oppressed,
>
> [19] to proclaim the year of the Lord's favor."

[20] And he rolled up the scroll and gave it back to the attendant and sat

down. And the eyes of all in the synagogue were fixed on him. [21] And

he began to say to them, "Today this Scripture has been fulfilled in your

hearing."

[22] And all spoke well of him and marveled at the gracious words that were coming from his mouth. And they said, "Is not this Joseph's son?" [23] And he said to them, "Doubtless you will quote to me this proverb, "'Physician, heal yourself." What we have heard you did at Capernaum, do here in your hometown as well.'"

[24] And he said, "Truly, I say to you, no prophet is acceptable in his hometown. [25] But in truth, I tell you, there were many widows in Israel in the days of Elijah, when the heavens were shut up three years and six months, and a great famine came over all the land, [26] and Elijah was sent to none of them but only to Zarephath, in the land of Sidon, to a woman who was a widow. [27] And there were many lepers in Israel in the time of the prophet Elisha, and none of them was cleansed, but only Naaman the Syrian."

[28] When they heard these things, all in the synagogue were filled with wrath. [29] And they rose up and drove him out of the town and brought him to the brow of the hill on which their town was built, so that they could throw him down the cliff. [30] But passing through their midst, he went away.

6. Jesus returns to Nazareth and seeks to teach those in his hometown. He begins by quoting the prophecy of Isaiah (61:1-2a). *How does Isaiah describe the ministry and impact of the coming Messiah?*

7. What are the implications of Jesus' statement in verse 21?

8. Put yourself in the synagogue as one who grew up with Jesus. What questions would you have had about Jesus, the hometown hero?

RELATE How It Applies to God / Life / You > Discuss

9. How would "childlike faith," rather than hostility, have better served those in Jesus' hometown?

10. Who is a "child" in your life who models faith? How could their childlike faith serve you well in your relationship with God?

NOTES on Study #4 | *Commentary and Historical Context*

Matthew 19:13-15; 18:1-5—Who's the greatest?

- The disciples can't seem to learn this lesson: Jesus is the champion of the weak. And in that society, indeed in all societies, the weakest members are the youngest. To him, children are not distractions; their rank makes them role models of living life as Jesus' followers. So, when a dispute arose about status, what better object lesson?!

Luke 4:14-30—Jesus Begins his Ministry

- A person did not necessarily need to have a special office to read Scripture aloud in a synagogue service, or to offer instruction. Jesus uses this occasion in his hometown to read from Isaiah and identify his ministry as a fulfillment of the prophet's vision of liberation. (See Isaiah 61:1-2).

- Jesus' reception turns as he claims the prophetic mantle of Elijah and Elisha, who suffered rejection in their homelands, but whose ministries helped "outsiders," such as the widow from Zarephath (1 Kings 17) and Naaman, the Syrian (2 Kings 5:1-19). Jesus' hometown cannot assume benefit from his ministry if they are unwilling to reconsider their view of him as merely an ordinary hometown kid.

REALISTIC *But* **REAL?** | *That's plausible but did it happen?*

Did Jesus hang out with children like this?
We have no record of Jesus befriending specific children, but such situations would not at all be surprising (Matthew 18:1-6; 19:13-15; 21:14-17).

Did Jesus camp out on his own, and later, with the disciples?
Again, we have no record of Jesus setting up a camp like this, but he did say, "The Son of Man has no place to lay his head" (Luke 9:58). We know he stayed in homes at times, but we do not know much about his housing situation or how often he camped out.

What is the "Shema" that the children recited?
The "Shema" is Deuteronomy 6:4-9 (including 11:13-21 and Numbers 15:37-41). It is a confession that faithful Jews recited twice daily. *Shema* is the word "hear" that begins Deuteronomy 6:4.

Did Jesus pray with such anguish to the Father?
He often withdraws from crowds to be alone with the Father (Mark 1:35) so this depiction is consistent with his practice of prayer.

HOME REFECTION | *Journaling, Commitments and Prayer*

Jesus encourages us to strive for his definition of greatness:

> *Whoever humbles himself like this child is the greatest in the kingdom of heaven.... And whoever would be great among you must be your servant* (Matthew 18:4; 28:26).

11. *How does "his formula" help you strive for greatness in your life?*

Video Insights: Jesus with Children –Dallas Jenkins
Type in URL: tinyurl.com/jesus-with-children (2:43 min.)

Notes: **Other Videos:**

After watching > discovering > relating, what slogan would you write or draw on your T-shirt?

Draft concepts:

Final design:

Another reminder

NOTE TO EVERYONE: *HOME REFLECTION.* Maybe you have not yet gotten to this section (as on pages 29-31, 39-41, and 51-53). No problem. Just don't miss this upcoming "at home" *Reflection* section (pages 71-73). The questions will help you deepen your relationship with God.

And, the *Real But Realistic* sections are nothing, if not entertaining!

The Rock on Which It Is Built

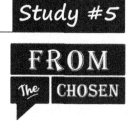

INTRO: In this episode, we meet fishing business owner **Zebedee,** and his two sons, **"Big"** James and **John** ("sons of Thunder" in Mark 3:17), along with several Pharisees and their students.

The **Pharisees** were a lay religious order who began around 160 BC, with good intentions of reviving Israel's adherence to Old Testament law. Unfortunately, by Jesus' day, those intentions had turned legalistic, as they followed their own traditions (see Mark 7:13) more than the Old Testament. Some have compared them to strict fundamentalists, in their legalistic concerns about dos and don'ts regarding Sabbath-keeping and other finer points of the Law.

WATCH View **Episode 4** (47 min., from 0:00 to 46:43) > **Discuss**

Simon lives in Capernaum on the sea of Galilee (see and mark the map, pages 138-139). In this episode he gets *caught up in his own net.* Before we read of the resolution in Luke 5, consider these questions: `

1. *How does the film depict Simon's crisis:*

   ... with the Romans/Quintus?

   ... with his brother, Andrew?

   ... with his wife, Eden?

   ... with God?

2. Nicodemus, too, is having a crisis. *What are the changes happening in his worldview and faith?*

DISCOVER Read Aloud > Mark It Up > Discuss

INTRO: Jesus had Simon's attention but now he was looking for a full commitment and vocational change with great purpose. If Jesus could make such a difference in Simon's life maybe there was hope for his contemporaries... and for us!

The Chosen takes liberties with the timeline from this passage. We have no indication from the gospels that Simon had a tax debt (see page 70). ***Underline all the action words by using a different color for each character.***

Jesus Heals Many and Calls Some

LUKE 4: [38] He left the synagogue and entered Simon's house. Simon's mother-in-law was ill with a high fever, and they appealed to him on her behalf. [39] And he stood over her and rebuked the fever, and it left her, and immediately she rose and began to serve them.

[40] When the sun was setting, all those who had any who were sick with various diseases brought them to him, and he laid his hands on every one of them and healed them. [41] And demons also came out of many, crying, "You are the Son of God!" But he rebuked them and did not allow them to speak, because they knew that he was the Christ....

LUKE 5: [1] On one occasion, while the crowd was pressing in on him to hear the word of God, he was standing by the lake of Gennesaret, [2] and he saw two boats by the lake, but the fishermen had gone out of them and were washing their nets. [3] Getting into one of the boats, which was Simon's, he asked him to put out a little from the land. And he sat down and taught the people from the boat.

[4] And when he had finished speaking, he said to Simon, "Put out into the deep and let down your nets for a catch."

[5] And Simon answered, "Master, we toiled all night and took nothing! But at your word I will let down the nets."

[6] And when they had done this, they enclosed a large number of fish, and their nets were breaking. [7] They signaled to their partners in the other boat to come and help them. And they came and filled both the boats, so that they began to sink.

⁸ But when Simon Peter saw it, he fell down at Jesus' knees, saying, "Depart from me, for I am a sinful man, O Lord." ⁹ For he and all who were with him were astonished at the catch of fish that they had taken, ¹⁰ and so also were James and John, sons of Zebedee, who were partners with Simon.

And Jesus said to Simon, "Do not be afraid; from now on you will be catching men." ¹¹ And when they had brought their boats to land, they left everything and followed him.

3. In Luke 4:38-39, Simon had witnessed the healing of his mother-in-law, but apparently does not respond to Jesus at that time. *Why does he now?*

4. *Why do you think Simon reacted so strongly?*

5. Note the title change from "Master" (v. 5) to "Lord" (v. 8). *Why is coming to grips with Jesus being Lord (even of his fishing business) so frightening, even defeating to him?*

RELATE How It Applies to God / Life / You > Discuss

6. Where is Jesus in relation to "your fishing business"—defined as central issues in your life—job, family, future goals, relationships:
   a) nowhere in sight right now
   b) on the horizon
   c) approaching the boat
   d) one foot in, one foot out
   e) fully committed, all in

   ... Explain your self-evaluation:

NOTES on Study #5 Commentary and Historical Context

Luke 5:1-11—Receiving a Change of Vocation

- Simon sees his mother-in-law healed (Luke 4:38-44), so he knows of Jesus' power, though maybe he is not completely convinced.

- Jesus is a carpenter, and Simon, a fisherman. Jesus' instructions to recast their nets would make no sense to an experienced fisherman. Apparently, Simon needed Jesus' intervention in an aspect of his life in which he considered himself an expert.

- It could be asked: *What does sin have to do with a large haul of fish?* Simon now understands who he's dealing with and who he is in comparison. His response reminds us of Isaiah's personal encounter with God in the Temple. Upon experiencing God's glory, Isaiah declares: *Woe is me! For I am lost; for I am a man of unclean lips, and I dwell in the midst of a people of unclean lips; for my eyes have seen the King, the Lord of hosts!* (see Isaiah 6:1-9).

- Like Isaiah, Simon (now called Peter in v. 8) is given a calling—one that is a grand vocation: to join Jesus as a "fisher of men." Fear is not appropriate, given that he has now united in purpose with Jesus.

REALISTIC

But REAL?

That's plausible but did it happen?

Did John the Baptist call the Pharisees "snakes"?
Yes, a "brood of vipers," in fact (Luke 3:7). John was eventually thrown into prison by Herod, not the Romans (Matthew 14:1–12; Mark 6:14–29). We have no record of Nicodemus visiting him in prison.

Did the Romans hire Matthew to "spy" on Simon?
Doubtful. We know that Matthew collected taxes in the region of Galilee, where Simon and Andrew lived. We do not know if they knew each other before Jesus called them together, although it is possible.

Did Andrew try to convince Simon, his brother, about Jesus?
Yes: *The first thing Andrew did after meeting Jesus was to find his brother and tell him, 'We have found the Messiah!* (John 1:41). However, unlike the plot of *The Chosen*, Simon goes right away to Jesus, and Jesus changes his name to "Peter" (1:42).

Did Matthew witness the miraculous catch of fish?
We have no record of Matthew being among those who Jesus taught from the boat. (Nor do we know if he witnessed the healing of the paralytic.) However, he very likely encountered Jesus prior to his response of following Jesus when called from his tax booth.

What about *The Chosen*'s timeline regarding the disciples?
Simon and Andrew, along with other disciples, followed Jesus *before* the miraculous catch of fish recorded in Luke 5. So, although *The Chosen* depicts the catch as Simon's first meeting with Jesus, he had prior encounters. Likewise, *The Chosen* depicts his mother-in-law healed *after* the catch, but (spoiler alert for Episode 8), this took place *before* the catch (Mark 1:30-31).

We also have no indication in Scripture that Simon (renamed Simon *Peter* by Luke in v. 8) was motivated by a tax debt. Still, there is no doubt that he was transformed by the miraculous catch and, along with the other fishermen, commits to following Jesus wholeheartedly with the new vocation of drawing people to Jesus and his message.

HOME REFLECTION Journaling, Commitments and Prayer

7. Jesus offers Simon a new vocation—catching people—and invites him to go "all in." *What would it take for you to "join Jesus" in a similar, all-in way? Be specific.*

8. Jesus also gives Simon a word of encouragement: "Do not be afraid" (v.10). *If you personalize Jesus' words, what do they mean to you in making an all-in commitment to him?*

Video Insights: Six Things You Didn't Know about Peter

Type in URL: tinyurl.com/info-on-peter –Brandon Robbins

Notes: *Other Videos?* (16:57 min.)

After watching > discovering > relating, what slogan would you write or draw on your T-shirt?

Draft concepts:

Final design:

 *Getting ready now for your last gathering.*

Please read the "Prior" note on page 118 (and its reference on page 15) regarding a longer event or retreat for Study #10.

If you haven't already done so, work on plans for your last gathering, to get it on your group members' schedules, if different than your normal meeting time.

The Wedding Gift

INTRO: It would be fascinating to know more about Jesus growing up in Nazareth with a humble, gracious mother, a God-fearing carpenter for a dad, and at least six siblings—four named brothers and at least two unnamed sisters (Matthew 13:55-56).

Of course, given the Bible's description of the Holy Spirit's involvement in Mary's pregnancy, they would be Jesus' half-brothers and sisters— same mother, different fathers! And, it should be noted, that Catholic tradition suggests Jesus' siblings were actually "cousins," or relatives, or possibly children from a first marriage of Joseph.

Regardless of your view on Jesus' family, everything the Bible tells us about his growing up years is found in one short passage: Luke 2:40-52.

Use your pen to follow the progression in this passage with a special focus on the words "and" and "when."

DISCOVER Read Aloud > Mark It Up > Discuss

The Boy Jesus in the Temple

LUKE 2: [40] The child grew and became strong, filled with wisdom. And the favor of God was upon him.

[41] Jesus' parents went to Jerusalem every year at the Feast of the Passover. [42] And when he was twelve years old, they went up according to custom.

[43] And when the feast was ended, as they were returning, the boy Jesus stayed behind in Jerusalem. His parents did not know it, [44] but supposing him to be in the group they went a day's journey, but then they began to search for him among their relatives and acquaintances, [45] and when they did not find him, they returned to Jerusalem, searching for him. [46] After three days they found him in the temple, sitting among the teachers, listening to them and asking them questions. [47] And all who heard him were amazed at his understanding and his answers.

[48] And when his parents saw him, they were astonished. And his mother said to him, "Son, why have you treated us so? Behold, your father and I have been searching for you in great distress." [49] And he said to them, "Why were you looking for me? Did you not know that I must be in my Father's house?" [50] And they did not understand the saying that he spoke to them.

[51] And he went down with them and came to Nazareth and was submissive to them. And his mother treasured up all these things in her

heart. [52] And Jesus increased in wisdom and in stature and in favor with God and man.

1. All parents can identify with the panic that comes from losing a child in a crowd. *What do you find surprising about this story?*

2. *What else do you learn about Jesus' parents and him as a boy?*

WATCH **View Episode 5** *(53 min., from 1:48 –54:24)* **> Discuss**

INTRO: **John the Baptist** languishes in prison, giving **Nicodemus** an opportunity to question him. (For more on John, see pages 28, 70 and 134.) This time it is about *miracles*—an interview  that began in Episode 4. Maybe John knows something about the source of this person and the power that does things he cannot un-see.

In the aftermath of the fish miracle, Eden finds out from her husband, Simon, about a new call on his life and lends her support. This is followed by a water-into-wine miracle. This miracle saved wine stewards, **Thomas** (a future disciple) and **Ramah** (a fictitious character in *The Chosen*), from dreadful humiliation at a wedding party. (For more on Thomas, see pages 82 and 135.)

3. What is Nicodemus's question, and John the Baptist's answer regarding apparent miracles?

4. How did Simon describe the miracle he had witnessed?

5. Why do you think Eden is so affirming of Simon's new calling to follow Jesus?

DISCOVER | Read Aloud > Mark It Up > Discuss

INTRO: *The Chosen's* version of the water-into-wine miracle contains plenty of lighthearted moments: tension between the bride's relatively poor family and the groom's rich parents, Jesus  playing with children, the disciples telling stories about how they first met Jesus, and the astonishment of those who saw the miracle.

The account we find in John's Gospel is much more concise. Of course, John could have "played it up," but his straightforward style lends credence to his integrity as an author of historical events. *The Chosen* is "happy" to embellish his just-the-facts narrative, and we are happy to study the source while engaging our imagination as well. ***Observe this interaction by highlighting the words spoken by each character.***

The Wedding at Cana

JOHN 2: On the third day there was a wedding at Cana in Galilee, and the mother of Jesus was there. [2] Jesus also was invited to the wedding with his disciples. [3] When the wine ran out, the mother of Jesus said to him, "They have no wine."

[4] And Jesus said to her, "Woman, what does this have to do with me? My hour has not yet come."

[5] His mother said to the servants, "Do whatever he tells you."

[6] Now there were six stone water jars there for the Jewish rites of purification, each holding twenty or thirty gallons.

[7] Jesus said to the servants, "Fill the jars with water." And they filled them up to the brim.

[8] And he said to them, "Now draw some out and take it to the master of the feast."

So they took it. [9] When the master of the feast tasted the water now become wine and did not know where it came from (though the servants who had drawn the water knew), the master of the feast called the bridegroom [10] and said to him, "Every-one serves the good wine first, and when people have drunk freely, then the poor wine. But you have kept the good wine until now."

[11] This, the first of his signs, Jesus did at Cana in Galilee, and manifested his glory. And his disciples believed in him.

[12] After this he went down to Capernaum, with his mother and his brothers and his disciples, and they stayed there for a few days.

6. What do you find unusual about this miracle?

7. How would you describe Jesus' interaction with his mother?

8. What effects did the miracle have on those who were there—the wedding party, servants, master of the feast, Mary (Jesus' mother), the disciples, Jesus?

9. Why do you think Jesus used his divine power to produce such ordinary things such as wine for a wedding, or fish for livelihood?

RELATE How It Applies to God / Life / You > Discuss

10. *What has God used to get your attention regarding spiritual things?*

NOTES on Study #6 Commentary and Historical Context

Luke 2:40-52—The Boy Jesus in the Temple

- Notice the artistic connection made in this episode where the boy Jesus and his mother both state, rhetorically: "If not now, when?" It's a nice touch and it won't be the last time those words are spoken between them. Yes, we're talking about the end of Season Two!

- Some have wondered how Jesus, who is God, could *grow* (as v. 52 indicates he did)? Jesus, as a human being, needed to grow and mature as all humans do. He had to learn such things as how to walk, speak, read, write and work. He just did so sinlessly!

John 2:1-12—The Wedding at Cana

- In Jewish culture a wedding was seen as uniquely sanctioned by God and thus worthy of the best of all parties where, hopefully, nothing ruinous happened, such as running out of wine!

- At this wedding in Cana, just a few miles from Jesus' hometown of Nazareth, Jesus becomes, in effect, Mary's "plus one," since her husband, Joseph, had likely passed away by this time.

- Jesus addresses Mary as "Woman," but is not discourteous; the word has no easy English equivalent. A phrase like, "My lady," better captures the respect behind its use here. Jesus' hesitation communicates they have a new relationship now, and that a public miracle is not a decision he will be pressured into performing.

REALISTIC But REAL?

That's plausible but did it happen?

Did Jesus' entire family get invited to the wedding in Cana?

Cana is close to Nazareth and Capernaum (John 2:12; see map on pages 138-139). Given this, Jesus' entire family may have attended. If so, the miracle did not convince them he was someone different than the person they knew growing up. Throughout his lifetime, they remain unconvinced of his identity (Mark 3:21; John 7:2-5).

Did Jesus ever build a privy (toilet)?
Possibly, given his previous occupation. He was a carpenter (Mark 6:3) who learned his trade from his dad (Matthew 13:55). The Greek word for *carpenter* can also be translated *craftsman* or *artisan*.

All the items that he made added value to others—from the *ordinary* to the *extraordinary*. Jesus may have made toy boats for children and lock-and-key inserts for doors (as depicted in the film version of reality). And he did the extraordinary by turning water into wine and, in the not-too-distant future, producing a couple of boatloads of fish!

Would running out of wine have been that embarrassing?
Yes. The show sets up the rich family/poor family wedding which serves to add a degree of drama, but such an event would have been humiliating, and a bad way to start a marriage! The guests often traveled for miles to attend, and such parties could last for days.

Did Thomas (and Ramah) serve wine at the wedding?
We have no record of Thomas serving at Cana, nor being called to follow Jesus there. The film's portrayal of Thomas as a "measurer" and "doubter" is consistent with one who later becomes known as "doubting Thomas" (John 11:16; 14:5-6; 20:24-29). *The Chosen* created the characters of Ramah (the wine steward) and Kafni (her father and vineyard owner), who add a colorful dimension to the story's account.

HOME REFLECTION *Journaling, Commitments and Prayer*

11. We all find ourselves wanting miracles in the ordinary course of our lives. *What is something you would like Jesus to do for you?*

12. *When God does not provide the miracle or outcome you desire, how have you, at times, processed disappointment in him?*

13. *By contrast, how would you like to process that disappointment?*

Video Insights: The Chosen Visits Wedding Miracle Site
Type in URL: tinyurl.com/the-wedding-site (4:03 min.) –Dallas Jenkins

Notes: **Other Videos:**

After watching > discovering > relating,
what slogan would you write or draw on your T-shirt?

Draft concepts:

Final design:

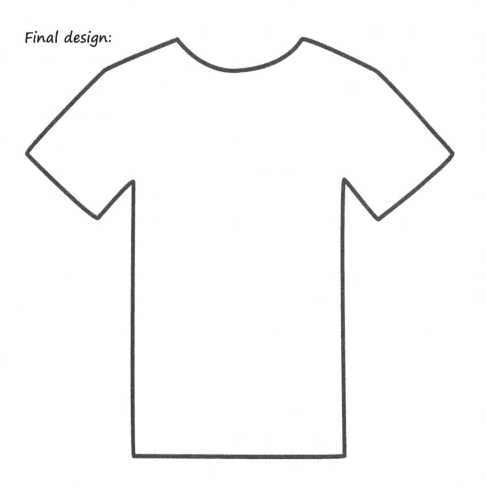

Getting ready for Study #7

NOTE FOR EVERYONE: It is helpful to google: *the names Jesus used for himself.* Such a search will turn up many—nearly 20, not to mention ones that others used to address him, plus those in the book of Revelation, totaling nearly 50.

Besides "Rabbi" and "Teacher," the most common title people used to describe Jesus in the New Testament was *Christ* (Greek for *Messiah*). But Jesus himself almost never used that designation, maybe because his general listeners had such misconceptions of who the Messiah would be. Instead, he preferred the title, *Son of Man.*

Some mistakenly assume this self-designation refers to the human side of Jesus; conversely, *Son of God* designates the divine side. Rather, as Jesus' audience would know, this title *(Son of Man)* is given to the heavenly, Messianic being envisioned in Daniel 7:13-14:

The Son of Man Is Given Dominion

DANIEL 7 [13] "I saw in the night visions,
and behold, with the clouds of heaven
    there came one like a **son of man**,
and he came to the Ancient of Days
    and was presented before him.

[14] And to him was given dominion
    and glory and a kingdom,
that all peoples, nations, and languages
    should serve him;
his dominion is an everlasting dominion,
    which shall not pass away,
and his kingdom one
    that shall not be destroyed.

Indescribable Compassion

INTRO: Many Jewish leaders were shocked by, and did not understand the ministry of John the Baptist. Isaiah 40:3-5 will be read in this episode and makes John's role clear. He will be the one who prepares the way for the coming of the Messiah.

When the Messiah shows up in first-century Israel, he acts like and does the very things that the Old Testament foretold about what the Messiah would be like and do. As an example, note how the upcoming miracle stories fulfill the description of the Messiah in Luke 4:18-19 (see page 58).

Use your pen to identify the things that are going to happen.

DISCOVER Read Aloud > Mark It Up > Discuss

Prepare the Way

ISAIAH 40: ³ A voice cries:

> "In the wilderness prepare the way of the Lord;
>
> > make straight in the desert a highway for our God.
>
> ⁴ Every valley shall be lifted up,
>
> > and every mountain and hill be made low;
>
> the uneven ground shall become level,
>
> > and the rough places a plain.
>
> ⁵ And the glory of the Lord shall be revealed,
>
> > and all flesh shall see it together,
>
> > for the mouth of the Lord has spoken."

1. What do Isaiah's analogies tell you about John the Baptist and his mission?

WATCH *View Episode 6 (50 min., from 0:00 to 49:48) > Discuss*

INTRO: Salome is introduced. She is Zebedee's wife and ends up in Jesus' inner circle. Likewise, Eden's mother (Simon's mother-in-law), **Dasha**, makes an appearance and is very sick. Before Season One's conclusion, she will meet Jesus in an unusual way!

Tamar (the Egyptian woman) is not mentioned in the Gospels. The show, however, follows the actual events and certainly fleshes out the emotions that those caught up in the story would have experienced.

2. As Jesus' ministry goes public, how does this episode describe:

... Matthew and what he has seen?

... the Pharisees' view of John the Baptist and their rigid view of God?

... Nicodemus witnessing the paralytic's healing?

DISCOVER   Read Aloud > Study > Discuss

INTRO: Leprosy is a debilitating and disfiguring nerve disease. It can now be cured, but in pre-scientific Israel, it was misunderstood and feared. In fact, the rabbis said it was easier to raise the  dead than to cure leprosy. This leper, like the paralytic described next had no hope of a cure, and was rejected by society (Leviticus 13:46) . *Ask the "W" questions (see page 12) and look for cause and effect.*

Jesus Cleanses a Leper
MARK 1: [40] And a leper came to him, imploring him, and kneeling said to him, "If you will, you can make me clean."

[41] Moved with pity, he stretched out his hand and touched him and said to him, "I will; be clean." [42] And immediately the leprosy left him, and he was made clean.

[43] And Jesus sternly charged him and sent him away at once, [44] and said to him, "See that you say nothing to anyone, but go, show yourself to the priest and offer for your cleansing what Moses commanded, for a proof to them." [45] But he went out and began to talk freely about it, and

to spread the news, so that Jesus could no longer openly enter a town, but was out in desolate places, and people were coming to him from every quarter.

Jesus Heals a Paralytic

MARK 2 And when he returned to Capernaum after some days, it was reported that he was at home. [2] And many were gathered together, so that there was no more room, not even at the door. And he was preaching the word to them. [3] And they came, bringing to him a paralytic carried by four men. [4] And when they could not get near him because of the crowd, they removed the roof above him, and when they had made an opening, they let down the bed on which the paralytic lay. [5] And when Jesus saw their faith, he said to the paralytic, "Son, your sins are forgiven."

[6] Now some of the scribes were sitting there, questioning in their hearts, [7] "Why does this man speak like that? He is blaspheming! Who can forgive sins but God alone?"

[8] And immediately Jesus, perceiving in his spirit that they thus questioned within themselves, said to them, "Why do you question these things in your hearts? [9] Which is easier, to say to the paralytic, 'Your sins are forgiven,' or to say, 'Rise, take up your bed and walk'? [10] But that you may know that the Son of Man has authority on earth to forgive sins"—he said to the paralytic— [11] "I say to you, rise, pick up your bed, and go home." [12] And he rose and immediately picked up his bed and went out before them all, so that they were all amazed and glorified God, saying, "We never saw anything like this!"

3. *What strikes you about these back-to-back miracles?*

4. The leper fails to follow Jesus' instructions. *How does that failure impact Jesus' future ministry?*

5. Jesus pronounces the paralytic forgiven and then uses the title, "Son of Man." *How do the Scribes react to this claim and why?*

RELATE How It Applies to God / Life / You > Discuss
_____

6. *How has your view of Jesus matured through the years?*

7. *In what ways do you still struggle in trusting him to come through for you?*

NOTES on Study #7 Commentary and Historical Context

Isaiah 40:3-5—Prepare the Way

- Leaving the cities for the wilderness is an exercise in purging oneself from distractions. As a word picture, the metaphor of building a road in rough terrain is like the preparation one makes to get ready for God's appearance. It is the very role that John the Baptist took on for the people of Israel, to prepare for Jesus' coming.

Mark 1:40—2:12—Jesus Cleanses and Heals

- Jesus wants the leper's witness to God's power proclaimed through the normal dictates of the Old Testament for such a healing. The second story not only identifies Jesus' power over sickness and disease, but it also reveals that this power is divine. This is shown by the disdain of Scribes (religious lawyers) for Jesus' claim that he can do what only God can do—forgive sins. For this alleged "blasphemy," they "call him out."

That's plausible but did it happen?

Did the catch of fish satisfy Simon/Andrew's taxes? We have no indication from Mark's Gospel that these fishermen/disciples had tax debts and we shouldn't read this into their motivations. But this high-value haul likely went to Simon's and the others' families to financially sustain them in their absence while traveling with Jesus.

Did Jesus grow up in Egypt and speak Egyptian?

Joseph and Mary fled to Egypt to avoid the massacre of baby boys under Herod (Matthew 2:13-15). Then they returned to Nazareth after Herod's death (2:19-23). They probably lived in Egypt for several years, though there is no evidence that he spoke Egyptian as an adult.

Hebrew was the language spoken in Jewish scholarly and religious circles and, undoubtedly, Jesus knew Hebrew. However, the common tongue spoken in the villages was a much more wide-spread Semitic one, Aramaic. Jesus also could have spoken *Koine* Greek and some Latin. Like most of his contemporaries, he would have been bilingual.

Did the Pharisees sell out John the Baptist to the Romans?
No. John confronted Herod Antipas regarding his illicit relationship with his brother's wife, Herodias. This so angered Herodias, that Herod imprisoned John and, at an opportune moment, Herodias appealed for his execution (Matthew 14:1-12; Mark 6:14-29; Luke 9:7-9).

Did Joseph die before Jesus began his ministry?
Probably, as there's no mention of him after Jesus begins his adult ministry. Joseph is last named in Luke's narration about the boy Jesus in the Temple (Luke 2:48; see on page 76-77).

Was Jesus constantly teaching God's truth in the form of parables?
Jesus told stories and parables more than once. He did so even more intentionally after he was further rejected (Matthew 13:10-17).

Did Nicodemus ask Mary for a meeting with Jesus?
Not likely, but we do know that it happened at night (John 3:2).

HOME REFLECTION *Journaling, Commitments and Prayer*

8. The Gospel passage and film episode stir up a lot of emotion. *How were you touched by it?*

... What do you sense Jesus is telling you about your life-condition?

Video Insights: The Son of Man –The Bible Project

Type in URL: tinyurl.com/son-of-man (5:50 min.)

Notes: Other Videos:

After watching > discovering > relating, what slogan would you write or draw on your T-shirt?

Draft concepts:

Final design:

 **Getting ready for your last gathering.**

Okay, we won't bother you anymore after this, but please read the "Prior" note on page 118 (and its reference on pages 15-16 regarding a longer event or retreat as an alternative for Study #10.

If you haven't already done so, finalize your plans for your last gathering to get it on your group members' schedules, if it is different than your normal meeting time.

Invitations

INTRO: Jesus explains his identity and purpose to Nicodemus in a unique way. He compares himself to a bronze serpent God had instructed Moses to fashion. This was the means God used to bring healing to the rebellious Israelites during an unusual incident in their 40-year exodus from Egypt.

When Moses lifted the bronze snake up on a pole, those who had been bitten by poisonous vipers could look up at it and be healed. This foreshadows the great redemption Jesus would bring when he, too, would be lifted up on a cross.

Identify the comparisons between these two passages.

The Bronze Serpent

NUMBERS 21: [4] From Mount Hor they set out by the way to the Red Sea, to go around the land of Edom. And the people became impatient on the way. [5] And the people spoke against God and against Moses, "Why have you brought us up out of Egypt to die in the wilderness? For there is no food and no water, and we loathe this worthless food."

[6] Then the Lord sent fiery serpents among the people, and they bit the people, so that many people of Israel died. [7] And the people came to Moses and said, "We have sinned, for we have spoken against the Lord and against you. Pray to the Lord, that he takes away the serpents from us." So, Moses prayed for the people.

[8] And the Lord said to Moses, "Make a fiery serpent and set it on a pole, and everyone who is bitten, when he sees it, shall live." [9] So Moses made a bronze serpent and set it on a pole. And if a serpent bit anyone, he would look at the bronze serpent and live.

Lifting Up the Son of Man

JOHN 3: [14] And as Moses lifted up the serpent in the wilderness, so must the Son of Man be lifted up, [15] that whoever believes in him may have eternal life.

1. Describe the story in Numbers 21 and the analogy in John 3.

2. The serpent on the pole has come to represent the curative power of medicine. *What does it refer to in these passages?*

WATCH View Episode 7 (35 min., from 0:00-35:11) > Discuss

INTRO: In the film, Moses' successor, **Joshua,** protests the serpent imagery, to which Moses says he's only doing as God instructs. The serpent on the pole, once looked at, will save the  Israelites from deadly snake bites. So also, Jesus will save his people he is lifted up on the Cross and they place their faith in him.

3. *Describe the struggle between:*

... *Nicodemus and his wife, Zohara?*

... *Matthew and his mother?*

... *Simon and Jesus, regarding Matthew?*

DISCOVER Read Aloud > Mark It Up > Discuss

INTRO: What follows is one of the weightiest passages in Scripture, indeed one of the most significant conversations in human history. Nicodemus was more than a devoted Pharisee; he was one of only 70 elite members of the Sanhedrin court.

He knew that Jesus was no ordinary man, but he was unsure what to make of him. Little did Nicodemus know of the transcendent nature of this conversation. It would provide not only for him, but the entire world, in all generations to come, the most insightful way to understand our relationship with God. *Ask the "W" questions (see page 12) and identify the analogies—similarities made to convey a point.*

You Must Be Born Again

JOHN 3 [1] Now there was a man of the Pharisees named Nicodemus, a ruler of the Jews. [2] This man came to Jesus by night and said to him, "Rabbi, we know that you are a teacher come from God, for no one can do these signs that you do unless God is with him."

[3] Jesus answered him, "Truly, truly, I say to you, unless one is born again he cannot see the kingdom of God."

[4] Nicodemus said to him, "How can a man be born when he is old? Can he enter a second time into his mother's womb and be born?"

[5] Jesus answered, "Truly, truly, I say to you, unless one is born of water and the Spirit, he cannot enter the kingdom of God. [6] That which is born of the flesh is flesh, and that which is born of the Spirit is spirit. [7] Do not marvel that I said to you, 'You must be born again.' [8] The wind blows where it wishes, and you hear its sound, but you do not know where it comes from or where it goes. So it is with everyone who is born of the Spirit."

[9] Nicodemus said to him, "How can these things be?"

[10] Jesus answered him, "Are you the teacher of Israel and yet you do not understand these things? [11] Truly, truly, I say to you, we speak of what we know, and bear witness to what we have seen, but you do not

receive our testimony. ^{12} If I have told you earthly things and you do not believe, how can you believe if I tell you heavenly things? ^{13} No one has ascended into heaven except he who descended from heaven, the Son of Man. ^{14} And as Moses lifted up the serpent in the wilderness, so must the Son of Man be lifted up, ^{15} that whoever believes in him may have eternal life.

For God So Loved the World

^{16} "For God so loved the world, that he gave his Son, that whoever believes in him should not perish but have eternal life. ^{17} For God did not send his Son into the world to condemn the world, but in order that the world might be saved through him. ^{18} Whoever believes in him is not condemned, but whoever does not believe is condemned already, because he has not believed in the name of the only Son of God. ^{19} And this is the judgment: the light has come into the world, and people loved the darkness rather than the light because their works were evil. ^{20} For everyone who does wicked things hates the light and does not come to the light, lest his works should be exposed. ^{21} But whoever does what is true comes to the light, so that it may be clearly seen that his works have been carried out in God."

4. Even though very familiar with the Old Testament, and though he knew of Jesus' miracles (v. 2), Nicodemus is baffled by Jesus. *What about Jesus' message is difficult for him?*

5. The term "born again" describes the transformation Nicodemus has not yet experienced, but very much needs. *What is the point of this analogy?*

6. *What does Jesus say are the results for those who are "born again," and for those who are not?*

7. *How does the new birth analogy contradict the idea that you can obtain God's approval through your religious performance?*

8. "Whoever" is used five times in vv. 15-21. *In what ways does God invite us to be included in his love, his light, and his life?*

RELATE How It Applies to God / Life / You > Discuss

9. Jesus turns every world religious system on its head, including Nicodemus', by insisting that God's love is unearned. That love is freely given but can only be experienced by faith in him. *In what way has God opened, or is opening your eyes to this truth?*

10. God's healing from sin is a freely given gift. *What about that truth is both difficult, and appealing, for you?*

NOTES on Study #8 Commentary and Historical Context

NUMBERS 21:4-9—The Bronze Serpent

- Complaining to God is not condemned in Scripture; it's celebrated. In the Psalms, we see testy, honest exchanges where David calls God to account. The Israelites had seen God's miraculous redemption in the plagues, pillar of fire, and manna from heaven. But they went beyond *complaining* to *condemning*. To speak "against God and against Moses" went too far. Hence, the Jewish people experienced God's punishment, but he also provides for their redemption. All they need to do is "look up."

- Going deeper, Numbers 21:4-9 acts as a bridge between Genesis 3:15 and John 3:14-15. Genesis 3:15 describes the snake bite which bruises the heel of God's Messiah-Redeemer (who then crushes the snake's head). John identifies the snake on the pole as Jesus' act of *crushing the biting snakes' heads* (John 3:14-15)—an act ending with his death and resurrection and the redemption of his people.

JOHN 3:1-15—You Must Be Born Again

- Whether to avoid the crowds and distractions, or the midday heat, or maybe to keep his reputation intact, Nicodemus meets Jesus at night.

- Jesus cuts to the chase, confronting Nicodemus (and us) about the need for a relationship with God based on a new, born-again nature. Opinions vary concerning what is meant by "born of water," but this statement parallels a natural, fleshly birth. A spiritual rebirth is likened to the wind: invisible but undeniable in its effects. Jesus' statement confronts anyone who thinks they can earn or merit the new birth through their own worthiness. Such a gift is to be *marveled in*—not so much to *marvel at* (v. 7).

JOHN 3:16-21—For God So Loved the World

- The leaders of Israel expect the Messiah to deal with the Romans, but Jesus would deal with sin and its tragic consequences. Sin destroys lives by separating us from God, from each other, and even from our very selves. Jesus succinctly lays out his place in God's plan, a plan that flows from one magnificent source: "For God so loved."

 **That's plausible but did it happen?**

Did Quintus express concern to Nicodemus about Jesus?
There is no "Quintus" identified in the Bible, although there are Roman magistrates and centurions like him. The Gospels do identify plenty of political tension during the time of Jesus' ministry, but no such dialogue with Nicodemus.

Was Matthew rejected by his parents?
The Gospels do not comment on Matthew's parents or their attitude toward him, but the portrayal of him as a traitor is how fellow Jews and his family would have viewed him.

Did Nicodemus himself eventually become "born again"?
Yes, that seems likely, as we see Nicodemus unashamedly identifying with Jesus again, later in the Gospel of John (7:45-52; 19:38-42).

Did Matthew leave immediately when Jesus said, "Follow me"?
Matthew (9:9), Mark (2:14), and Luke (5:27-28) tell us that Matthew left everything. *The Chosen* portrays the drama of his readiness in that moment! What led up to his *immediate decision* is not identified.

Did Simon initially reject the idea of Matthew joining their group?
We have no record of this. But "antiestablishment" types, such as fisherman Simon, and "establishment" types, such as tax collector Matthew, were bound to be at odds. They would have been all the more so as Matthew was considered a traitor to the Jewish nation.

Jesus knew that learning to value and care for each other would help prepare the disciples to minister to the diverse people they would meet. It's like he planned on calling 12 *mismatched* disciples! *The Chosen* and the Gospels increasingly portray differences over issues that brought conflict between the disciples. What they had in common was their relationship to Jesus. Sounds similar to us!

HOME REFLECTION *Journaling, Commitments and Prayer*

11. John 3:16 is probably the most well-known verse in the Bible. *What does John 3:16 mean to you personally?* (Feel free to continue your thoughts on pages 106-107.)

Video Insights: Bringing John 3:16 to the Screen -Dallas Jenkins

Type in URL: tinyurl.com/filming-john3 (5:46 min.)

Notes: Other Videos:

After watching > discovering > relating,
what slogan would you write or draw on your T-shirt?

Draft concepts:

Final design:

 **What is your favorite Chosen episode so far?**

NOTE TO EVERYONE: Of course, there's a wide difference of opinion regarding the above question, but many pick this final episode. Regardless, because of its length, you might want to *first read over the passage on which the episode ends before beginning your study*: John 4:1-26 (see pages 111-113).

I Am He

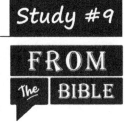

INTRO: Jesus had the uncomfortable propensity to associate with the wrong kind of people. For example, he attended a dinner party at Matthew's (a "tax collector and sinner's") house, and he engaged in conversation with an outcast woman from Samaria.

The next study (#10) will focus on the conversation Jesus has when the disciples return with food from Sychar (John 4:27-39). In this study, we will focus on Jesus' longest recorded conversation (John 4:1-26).

Identify who is involved and what contrasts are made between them.

DISCOVER | Read Aloud > Mark It Up > Discuss

Jesus Calls Matthew

Matthew 9 ⁹As Jesus passed on from there, he saw a man called Matthew sitting at the tax booth, and he said to him, "Follow me." And he rose and followed him.

¹⁰And as Jesus reclined at table in the house, behold, many tax collectors and sinners came and were reclining with Jesus and his disciples. ¹¹And when the Pharisees saw this, they said to his disciples, "Why does your teacher eat with tax collectors and sinners?" ¹²But when he heard it, he said, "Those who are well have no need of a physician, but those who are sick. ¹³Go and learn what this means: 'I desire mercy, and not sacrifice.' For I came not to call the righteous, but sinners."

1. *What is surprising about Jesus calling Matthew to follow him?*

...eating dinner with tax collectors and sinners?

2. *Why do you think tax collectors and sinners are drawn to Jesus?*

WATCH | View Episode 8 (51 min., from 2:01 to 52:41) > Discuss

The Chosen's episode begins and ends at the same well. The scene opens with a flashback to **Jacob and sons** digging and visited by a cynical neighbor. This well can be visited today. Jacob's twelve sons head up the original twelve tribes of Israel.

3. A major theme in this episode is being seen. *Who needs to be seen and how does Jesus assure them that they are being seen?*

4. *What prevents Nicodemus from following Jesus at this point?*

DISCOVER Read Aloud > Mark It Up > Discuss

NOTE: The Jews considered Samaritans as half-breed and religious inferiors, normally bypassed Samaria when traveling between Judea and Galilee. Not Jesus. (For more on this, see page 114.)
Look for and mark references to water and worship.

Jesus and the Samaritan Woman

JOHN 4 ¹ Now when Jesus learned that the Pharisees had heard that he was making and baptizing more disciples than John ² (though Jesus himself did not baptize, but only his disciples), ³ he left Judea and departed again for Galilee.

⁴ And he had to pass through Samaria. ⁵ So he came to a town of Samaria called Sychar, near the field that Jacob had given to his son Joseph. ⁶ Jacob's well was there; so Jesus, wearied as he was from his journey, was sitting beside the well. It was about the sixth hour.

⁷ A woman from Samaria came to draw water. Jesus said to her, "Give me a drink." ⁸ (For his disciples had gone away into the city to buy food.)

⁹ The Samaritan woman said to him, "How is it that you, a Jew, ask for a drink from me, a woman of Samaria?" (For Jews have no dealings with Samaritans.)

¹⁰ Jesus answered her, "If you knew the gift of God, and who it is that is saying to you, 'Give me a drink,' you would have asked him, and he would have given you living water."

¹¹ The woman said to him, "Sir, you have nothing to draw water with, and the well is deep. Where do you get that living water? ¹² Are you greater than our father Jacob? He gave us the well and drank from it himself, as did his sons and his livestock."

¹³ Jesus said to her, "Everyone who drinks of this water will be thirsty again, ¹⁴ but whoever drinks of the water that I will give him will never be thirsty again. The water that I will give him will become in him a spring of water welling up to eternal life."

¹⁵ The woman said "Sir, give me this water, so that I will not be thirsty or have to come here to draw water."

¹⁶ Jesus said to her, "Go, call your husband, and then come here."

¹⁷ The woman answered him, "I have no husband."

Jesus said to her, "You are right in saying, 'I have no husband'; ¹⁸ for you have had five husbands, and the one you now have is not really your husband. What you have said is true."

¹⁹ The woman responded to him, "Sir, I perceive that you are a prophet. ²⁰ Our fathers worshiped on this mountain, but you say that in Jerusalem is the place where people ought to worship."

²¹ Jesus said to her, "Woman, believe me, the hour is coming when neither on this mountain nor in Jerusalem will you worship the Father. ²² You worship what you do not know; we worship what we know,

for salvation is from the Jews. ²³ But the hour is coming, and is now here, when the true worshipers will worship the Father in spirit and truth, for the Father is seeking such people to worship him. ²⁴ God is spirit, and those who worship him must worship in spirit and truth."

²⁵ The woman said to him, "I know that the Messiah is coming (he who is called Christ). When he comes, he will tell us all things."

²⁶ Jesus said to her, "I who speak to you am he."

5. *What barriers (geographical, political, theological, social, gender) does Jesus break down by entering a conversation with the woman?*

6. *How does Jesus lead this conversation to the point of revealing his identity?*

7. *What does Jesus want to teach her about true worship?*

8. *What do you think finally opens her eyes to who Jesus is?*

RELATE How It Applies to God / Life / You > Discuss

9. *How do people seek to quench their thirst for hope and purpose?*

10. *Describe the first time you felt a thirst for what Jesus has to offer.*

NOTES on Study #9 Commentary and Historical Context

John 4:1-30—Having our Thirst Quenched

- Samaritans' and Jews' animosity toward each other can be traced back to the Assyrian invasion of Northern Israel in 721 AD. The conquerors took many Samaritan Jews into captivity. Foreigners repopulated and intermarried, altering the inhabitants' Judaism with other religious rites, even paganism (see 2 Kings 17:24-29).

  When Zerubbabel returned from exile to rebuild Jerusalem's temple, (between 538 and 520 BC), he spurned Samaritan help. Given their very different religious orientation, the Samaritans then sought to prevent the Temple from being rebuilt (Ezra 4:1-10). And they built their own temple on Mt. Gerizim, later destroyed by the Jews.

- Jesus is the master conversationalist. He breaks down conventions (male/female, Jew/Samaritan, rabbi/sinner), builds common ground, avoids diversion, and gets to the woman's real need. This conversation is a great example of how to build rapport, identify a person's need, and seek to meet it in a meaningful way.

- This woman is an outcast (comes to the well alone at noon, has had "five husbands,") and suffered much rejection. Jesus offers her *living water* to meet her deepest need—a relationship with himself. Jesus' offer is as radical as *living water* is to well water (see John 7:37-39).

That's plausible but did it happen?

Did Jacob dig a well that Jesus came to (and that still exists today)? Although there is no specific record of Jacob and sons digging a well, he came to Shechem, which is called Sychar in John 4, where he pitched a tent and built an altar (Genesis 33:18-20). The well in John 4 is called "Jacob's well," and tradition identifies him as having dug it

Was Simon Peter the only married disciple? Yes, as far as we know. Although it would be interesting to know about Simon's wife and their relationship as the show speculates, we have no biblical account beyond the fact that he had a mother-in-law and, thus, a wife!

HOME REFLECTION *Journaling, Commitments and Prayer*

11. A recurring theme has been people finding their needs met by Jesus—"Water for the Thirsty." *When you consider your greatest needs, what comes to mind?*

12. *In what ways has Jesus met your needs? (Or how have you considered trusting him more to do so?)*

Video Insights: The Chosen in Israel, Samaritan scene

Type in URL: tinyurl.com/woman-at-the-well –Dallas Jenkins

Notes: **Other Videos:**   (6:25 min.)

After watching > discovering > relating,
what slogan would you write or draw on your T-shirt?

Draft concepts:

Final design:

 Time to put it all together

-The tenth meeting includes a review of Season One, a bridge to Season Two, and reflection on what we've learned and experienced so far.

Note: For this gathering, your group could meet at your normal time, or as an alternative, you could plan to meet in a special place for a longer event which can do wonders as a group bonding experience. **Pages 127-132** can be used for an *extended Home Reflection* time, or for an All-Day *or Weekend gathering event.*

See page 15 for an overview of a **Day-Long Event** or **Weekend Retreat.** See thechosenstudy.org for further suggestions under *Leaders.*

It is a priority to have as many in your group come as possible, hopefully everyone, no matter what you do! So, discuss options and get it on your group members' schedule, as early as possible.

Hopefully, you and your group will continue the Chosen experience and invite new people to your next study!

-**For this study,** we use a *Bible Project* video and two film clips from Episode 8 (page 120).

Integrate Your Chosen Experience

Season One Reviewed and Looking Ahead   **Study #10**

INTRO: The cover on this guide illustrates the centrality of water in our lives. But of course, our thirst runs deeper. We have a "God-shaped void" only God himself can satisfy.

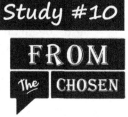

Jesus works hard to get his point across to the woman he meets at the well, later identified as **Photina**. He tells her that the source to quench such thirst comes only from a relationship with him. He will be her Messiah—the anointed, Servant-King, sent from God the Father.

Let's see how "water of life" carries through as a biblical theme. We can trace this source of life from Creation to this very encounter at Jacob's Well.

WATCH View *BibleProject.com, Water of Life* (4 min.) > Discuss
(tinyurl.com/water-of-life)

This video depicts the "water of life" image in the following scenes:

   ... the river in the Garden of Eden (Gen 2:5-6).
   ... the drought of the human condition.
   ... Jacob digs a well, restarting God's family.
   ... yet the desert/dry bones/thirst continues.
   ... the "woman at the well" story reimagined.
   ... Jesus' death on the cross as a fountain
   ... the climax of God's Spirit in us bringing life.

1. *When have you felt spiritually or emotionally "thirsty" (far from God, alone, betrayed, outcast)?*

2. *How has or could the "water of life," described in this video, impact your life?*

RE-WATCH View **Episode 8** (15 min. from 0:00 to 4:26 and from
40:08 to 50:48) > Discuss

3. Let's revisit the *living water* scene from this story. Even though the woman leaves her water jug at the well, she is no longer thirsty. How has Jesus satisfied her deepest needs?

4. While she came to the well as a woman of shame, she leaves as an emissary of restoration. *How do you imagine this turn of events will impact the woman and others in her hometown of Sychar?*

DISCOVER Read Aloud > Mark It Up > Discuss

INTRO: The disciples, having gone to town to find food, now return and offer some to Jesus. His response leaves them more confused. Jesus gets his hunger satisfied with something else. *Look for the priorities and how they're expressed by each of the characters.*

The Disciples Return

JOHN 4 [27] Just then his disciples came back. They marveled that he was talking with a woman, but no one said, "What do you seek?" or, "Why are you talking with her?"

[28] So the woman left her water jar and went into town and said to the people, [29] "Come, see a man who told me all that I ever did. Can this be the Christ?" [30] They went out of the town and were coming to him.

[31] Meanwhile the disciples were urging him, saying, "Rabbi, eat."

[32] But he said, "I have food to eat that you do not know about."

[33] So the disciples said to one another, "Has anyone brought him something to eat?"

[34] Jesus said to them, "My food is to do the will of him who sent me and to accomplish his work. [35] Do you not say, 'There are yet four months, then comes the harvest'? Look, I tell you, lift up your eyes.

See that the fields are white for harvest. [36] Already the one who reaps is receiving wages and gathering fruit for eternal life, so that sower and reaper may rejoice together. [37] For here the saying holds true, 'One sows and another reaps.' [38] I sent you to reap that for which you did not labor. Others have labored, and you have entered into their labor." [39] Many Samaritans from that town believed in him because of the woman's testimony, "He told me all that I ever did."

5. *What do the disciples find confusing about Jesus' words and actions?*

6. *What is the "living food" that Jesus is talking about and wants his disciples to have?*

7. *Compared to the expected harvest four months away, what kind of harvest timeframe does Jesus envision for him and his disciples?*

RELATE How It Applies to God / Life / You > Discuss

Jesus uses many metaphors in this passage. He enjoys *living food* as he provides *living water* to the woman and, through her, to her village. He then invites his disciples to participate in a *living harvest*.

8. *What is, or might be, difficult for you in responding to Jesus' invitation to become a reaper and harvester of people?*

9. *Which friends, neighbors, co-workers, and/or family members do you sense God would have you help (as salt and light) through service, prayer, and dialogue about spiritual things?*

-      -   -

-      -   -

-      -   -

10. *How might you use The Chosen Study as a means of inviting people into a dialogue about Jesus?*

11. *Could you imagine yourself going a step further by serving in a key role, even leading a group? If so, how could you take the next step?*

Note: Please consider *Our Mission—Our Team—Our Invitation* on page 155. We'd love to have you join with us: thechosenstudy.org/join.

NOTES on Study #10 Commentary and Historical Context

John 4:31-39—The Disciples Return

- Like *living water* that replenishes the spirit, there is *living food* that sustains the soul. The disciples completely miss the point in their focus on ordinary food, wondering if Jesus had already eaten.

- Many pursuits energize us. For Jesus, it is God's work in the lives of people that provides real satisfaction—forsaking small ambitions for the larger ambition of meeting people's deepest needs.

- Jesus' "food" comes in providing *living water* through the woman's word. This event lays the groundwork for a *living harvest* among the Samaritans, coming in Season Two. Check out John 4:39-42.

HOME REFLECTION Looking back and looking forward

12. **Read through pages 133-135.** These pages describe the Gospels' authors and characters. *What surprised, encouraged, or challenged you about their stories?*

    –

    –

    –

    –

13. *Where would you have placed yourself on this continuum (put a smaller x) regarding your relationship with God/Jesus when you began this study (see p. 39)? Where are you now (put a larger X)?*

    _____
    Observer...   Skeptic...   Learner...   Seeker...   Follower...

14. *What new spiritual perspective do you have about God/Jesus/ direction in your life/other?*

−

−

−

−

Video Insights: Woman at the Well   −Olivia Lane

Type in URL: tinyurl.com/woman-at-the-well-song (4:39 min.)

Notes: **Other Videos:**

After watching > discovering > relating, what slogan would you write or draw on your T-shirt?

Draft concepts:

Final design:

Your Faith Journey *Best takeaways for:*

- -An Extended Home Reflection
- -A Day-Long Event
- -A Weekend Retreat *(See page 15 for these.)*

#1, The Shepherd:

#2, I Have Called You by Name:

#3, Shabbat:

#4, Jesus Loves the Little Children:

#5, The Rock on Which it is Built:

More takeaways: (For longer events see website under Leaders.)

#6, The Wedding Gift:

#7, Indescribable Compassion:

#8, Invitations:

#9, I Am He:

#10, Integrate Your Chosen Experience:

Read this definition of faith and "Mark It Up!"

The Chosen is meant to take you into the eyes and ears of the people who followed Jesus. We believe that if you can see Jesus through the eyes of those who met him, you can be changed and impacted in the same way they were.... If we can connect you with their burdens and struggles and questions, then ideally, we can connect you to the solution, to the answer to those questions. ~Dallas Jenkins

One definition of genuine faith is *giving all you know about yourself to all you know about God.* Such is the call to humility. And the more you hang around Jesus, the more you realize that he isn't impressed with pretension. Maybe that's why he—the Servant-King, God's under-stated Messiah—made no grand entry. Instead, Jesus shows up as a baby, born in a dirty stable to a peasant girl, in a nondescript town.

Then, 30 years later, for three short years, he announces that the Kingdom of God has arrived, complete with spiritually intriguing stories and miracles. He offers forgiveness of sin, and reconciliation to God the Father—all culminating in his crucifixion, resurrection, and ascension.

Something is going on here. No one could make this stuff up. If nothing more, **the story of Jesus is the most [_____ fill in the blank] story that humanity has ever offered**. The Gospel writers certainly felt this way and their eagerness to describe this off-the-charts, unusual *eternity-meets-time event* pours through their various accounts.

*From your study, **write in the adjective** that best describes Jesus' story?*
　　Remarkable...
　　　　Compelling...
　　　　　　Audacious...
　　　　　　　　Captivating...
No fair picking them all!　　　　Fascinating...
We chose one—what's yours?　　　Intriguing...
Share why you selected it with your group.　　Other...

Watch > Discover > Relate the Most _____ Story Ever Told.

Do you increasingly find yourself caught up in Jesus' story, as well? Do you want it, and him, to influence your life more deeply? Then, take on what you learn. If Jesus says to love your enemies, try it out. Or, if he says to show hospitality like the Good Samaritan, or to help find lost sheep like a Good Shepherd, then do it.

As you "try on Jesus' teaching," you will find it not only making sense, but that you will also need to look to him for the wisdom, strength, and courage to take the risk of making some hard choices. Thankfully, in this journey of faith, his forgiveness is always close at hand.

1. *How have you connected with the above quote by Dallas?*

2. *How do you respond to the definition of faith given on page 129?*

3. *Which teaching of Jesus would God have you "try on" right now?*

4. *With whom can you share what you've learned and its impact on you?*

Faith Journey Notes:

Have you seen something different in Jesus?

Join a Chosen Study Team and consider becoming a

Chosen Study Leader

More Notes:

Background Notes Where his story came from

Early tradition identifies Matthew, Mark, Luke, and John as the ones who introduced Jesus to the First Century world and to ours. Their portrait of him is both historically unique and remarkably consistent.

MATTHEW: Given his occupation as a tax collector for the Roman government, we can only imagine the initial tension between Matthew (also called Levi) and the other disciples. But reconciliation lay at the heart of Jesus' message (see *The Sermon on the Mount,* Mathew 5-7). Matthew's Gospel emphasizes the interconnectedness between the Old and New Testaments and provides young believers a systematic tutorial on Jesus' teaching.

MARK: This Gospel has been generally recognized as the account coming from Peter. Mark begins his first "sentence" with no verb: *The beginning of the Gospel about Jesus Christ, the Son of God.* His last sentence ends with the women fleeing Jesus' empty tomb *because they were afraid.* For Mark, Jesus is a man of action. To help believers facing persecution from the Roman state, Mark focuses on Jesus as the Suffering Servant who "came to serve" (Mark 10:45).

LUKE: An educated Greek physician and traveling companion of Paul, Luke authored the book of Acts and the Gospel that bears his name. Although Luke never met Jesus himself, he had a close relationship with Paul, and was acquainted with most of the key eyewitnesses who knew Jesus (Luke 1:1-4). After extensive interviews with these contacts, Luke begins: "Since I myself have carefully investigated everything from the beginning, it seemed good also to me to write an orderly account" (Luke 1:3).

JOHN: A fisherman and brother of James, he writes, "In the beginning was the Word," offering a rather obvious parallel to the opening words of Genesis. In the "first Genesis," God spoke *Creation* into existence, and in the "second Genesis" God speaks *Redemption* into existence: "The Word became flesh and made his dwelling among us" (1:14). This "Word made flesh" is who John wants his readers to know.

Knowing those who knew him best

Mary Magdalene: She was one of several women mentioned in Luke 8:2-3, who had been "cured of evil spirits and diseases," and was following Jesus. Having been delivered from seven demons, she is with Jesus at the cross and is the first one to whom Jesus appears after the Crucifixion (Luke 8:2-3; John 19:25-27; John 20:1-18).

Nicodemus: As a Pharisee, he also ruled as a member of the Sanhedrin, the supreme religious council in Jerusalem during New Testament times. His encounter with Jesus in John 3 is the occasion for the well-known verse, John 3:16. He boldly steps up to help bury Jesus' body, with Joseph of Arimathea, post-crucifixion (John 3:1-21; 7:45-52; 19:38-42).

John the Baptist: Miraculously conceived shortly before his cousin Jesus, he heralds Jesus, as foretold by Isaiah (40:3-5), calling Jews to repent in preparation for the Messiah. After a faithful ministry, and baptizing Jesus, he is imprisoned and later beheaded for the threat he posed to Herod Antipas. Jesus identifies him as the "greatest of those born of women" (John 1:6-34; Matthew 3:1-17; 11:1-19; 14:1-12; Luke 1:5-25, 57-80).

Andrew: One of the first to follow Jesus, he brings his brother, Simon (Peter), right away. Together with fellow fishermen, James and John, Andrew leaves everything to follow Jesus after the miraculous catch. He also plays a key role in the feeding of the 5,000 (John 1:40-42; 6:8-9).

Simon: This fisherman meets Jesus and is later renamed Peter, *the Rock.* He is brought to Jesus by his brother, Andrew, and follows Jesus thereafter. He is well-known for walking (and sinking) on water, slicing off a soldier's ear, denying Jesus before his death, being a prominent leader in the early Christian movement, and for writing 1 and 2 Peter (Matthew 14:25-32; 16:13-28; Mark 14:66-72; John 1:40-42; Luke 5:1-11).

James and John: Along with Simon, they become Jesus' closest disciples. Appropriately nicknamed by Jesus as the "sons of thunder" (Luke 9:54), they were Simon's partners and, like him, they left everything to follow Jesus after the huge catch of fish (Mark 3:17; Luke 5:1-11). John goes on to write a Gospel, three letters, and the Book of Revelation.

Zebedee and **Salome** are the parents of James and John. Salome is named twice in Scripture and is highlighted several other times. Though not above asking favor for her two sons (Matthew 20:20-28), she is a devoted follower of Jesus. She is there at his crucifixion (Mark 15:40) and the resurrection (Mark 16:1). (See also Matthew 20:20-28; Mark 10:35-40)

Matthew: Also known as Levi, he is a despised tax collector when Jesus calls him from his tax booth to follow Him. He "left everything and followed him," and invites many friends and coworkers to a dinner with Jesus (Luke 5:27-32). He authors the Gospel of Matthew.

James the Less (*micros,* meaning "little" or "young") and **Thaddeus**: Two lesser-known disciples. "Little James," a son of Alphaeus (Mark 3:18), could have been Matthew's brother (also a son of Alphaeus, Mark 2:14), but never identified as such. Thaddeus, aka Jude/Judas, may have gotten his nickname (meaning "breast child" or "mama's boy") to distinguish him from the other Judas, whose name carries negative connotations.

Thomas (aka Didymus, or "twin"): Best known for doubting: *Unless I see the nail marks in his hands... I will not believe* (John 20:25). Thomas could, maybe more accurately, be called *logical*. Regardless, we see a whole-hearted passion, even an openness to die with Jesus (11:16), and fear of missing him (14:5). Thomas, the last of The Twelve to see Jesus after the resurrection, upon seeing him proclaims, *My Lord and my God* (20:24-29).

Mary, mother of Jesus: She is the teenager God chose to give birth to Jesus, who was conceived in her by the Holy Spirit. She raises Jesus from birth, along with **Joseph**. Joseph marries her after an angel appears to him in a dream; he probably died before Jesus began his adult ministry. Mary weeps at the Crucifixion, witnesses the resurrected Christ and, along with at least some of her other children (Acts 1:14), is part of the early church (Luke 1:26-56; 2:5-7; 8:19-21; John 2:1-12; 19:25-27).

The Leper: An outcast and "untouchable" in his society (Leviticus 13:46), this particular leper receives compassion and healing from Jesus. Even Jesus touching him would have been shocking, both to him and to any onlookers. He is only the first of many lepers and other social outcasts— the paralyzed, blind, lame, sick, and demon-possessed—that Jesus heals and cleanses (Matthew 8:2-4; Mark 1:40-45; Luke 5:12-16; 17:11-19).

Spoiler Alert! What happens next . . .

Episode 1: The opening scene not only sets the stage for Season Two, but it also serves as prologue for how the Gospels were written. Here we find **John** interviewing key witnesses, writing notes and musing with Jesus' mother, Mary, about how to begin his Gospel.

After Jesus encounters **Photina**, the Samaritan woman, he and his disciples visit her hometown of Sychar for two days (John 4:43). During this time, **James** and **John** till a field, and the disciples "lose" Jesus while he fixes a cart axle. Also, Photina's husband, among others, listens to Jesus tell the Parable of the Lost Sheep (Luke 15:1-7). The parable foreshadows a fascinating encounter with a "lost sheep," **Melech**, and an interesting reference to the Good Samaritan parable.

Episode 2: The disciples welcome **Philip**—a student of John the Baptist, and friend of Andrew. Now changing allegiance from John to Jesus, he seeks out his old friend, **Nathanael,** with whom he shares the good news. Nathanael (in this show, a failed architect) was despondent over a collapsed building and the loss of his career. But he finds new purpose in meeting and following the man who saw him under a fig tree.

Episode 3: No new characters, but crowds of people line up for healing. We listen in on compelling insights as the disciples, including Mother Mary, seek to understand the movement they have joined. Tensions rise as Simon and Andrew confront Matthew about his former life. But their arguments look petty as an exhausted Jesus returns, laboring as he walks through the camp to his tent.

Episode 4: Here we meet **Jesse**, permanently lame from a childhood accident until he is healed by Jesus some 38 years later (John 5:1-9). His brother in this show, **Simon the Zealot**—trained as an assassin, but stunned to see his brother healed—rejects his zealot vows to join this new movement. Jesus increasingly "stirs up the water," coming to the attention of the Roman authorities and Jewish religious leaders.

Episode 5: The older cousin by six months, **John the Baptist** and Jesus have a sit-down conversation. **Mary Magdalene** struggles with PTSD from a close encounter with a Roman soldier and a demon-possessed man called **Legion** (real name, **Caleb**), who is delivered by Jesus. She ends up drawn back into her old lifestyle and leaves the group, who are very concerned about her disappearance. Jesus is as well, and sends Simon and Matthew to look for and, hopefully, return her.

Episode 6: Mary falls deeper into old habits, but Simon and Matthew find her and bring her back. She meets with Jesus, who is quick to extend forgiveness. The focus on love over law, and recovery over re-lapse, stands in sharp contrast to the views of the Pharisees, **Shmuel** and **Yanni**. They seek to bring Jesus to 'justice' for what they see as blasphemy, for healings and grain-eating (harvesting) on the Sabbath.

Episode 7: Jesus and his disciples prepare for an upcoming sermon to be witnessed by thousands. But that scenario appears to blow up when Roman soldiers lead Jesus away to Capernaum for questioning before **Quintus** (the Roman Praetor from Season One) and one of Caesar's cohorts, **Atticus**, who has been tailing Jesus. Andrew, despondent over John's imprisonment, leaves the group along with Philip. They come upon the Egyptian woman, **Tamar**, and the healed paralytic—both speaking about Jesus while Jesus is wanted for questioning. The episode ends with Jesus returning and the disciples asking him to teach them how to pray in the same manner that he does. Their desire to get "the heart and the mind right" pleases Jesus.

Episode 8: We anticipate the Big Reveal, as Jesus and Matthew work together on what will be called the *Sermon on the Mount* (Matthew 5-7). Jesus comes up with just the right introduction (the Beatitudes), while the disciples busy themselves with finding and negotiating the right spot, preparing leaflets, inviting townsfolk, welcoming old friends, and parents—plus crowd control. Thousands gather, including one who finds himself caught up in it all, **Judas (Iscariot)**. Jesus, decked out in a blue "Prince of Peace" sash, finally takes to the stage, and... (hold the drum roll, please) the long-awaited Big Reveal will now be... delivered in Season Three.

Mark where it happened on the map (Bible-History.com)

Map of Israel in the New Testament

Bible History Online

Record locations cited and what happened there:

- Bethlehem Ephrathah: Micah 5:2 (p. 22) Jesus' birthplace

- Nazareth, Jesus' hometown: Luke 2:4 (p. 26)

- Bethlehem (City of David): Luke 2:4, 15 (p. 26-27)

-

-

-

-

-

Bible apps and online access

 The **You Version** app, installed on over 500 million devices, is used on smartphones and tablets, and accessed online at bible.com and youversion.com. Excellent for reading.

 Bible Gateway is a searchable online Bible in more than 200 versions and 70 languages that can be read and referenced online at biblegateway.com. Excellent for researching.

 BibleProject.com and app, used in studies #1 and #10, includes a quality collection of videos on books of the Bible, biblical themes, and word studies. Excellent for learning.

100% FREE: The Life and Teachings of Jesus of Nazareth

Would you like a compilation of the four Gospels for yourself and to give away? Order free (224 pages, shipping included) at plusnothing.com.

Can you trust The Chosen?

Some have raised questions about the authenticity of *The Chosen*—which is what this guide's *Realistic But Real?* sections highlight. An analogy to Bible translation could be made in this regard.

Some Bible translations strictly follow the original Hebrew and Greek, but such very literal renditions can make it difficult to read in other languages. Other translations focus on meaning by reworking sentence structures into a better, native-reading format: a "dynamic equivalent." (*The Chosen Study* uses one slightly tilted toward literal: ESV.)

Still other "translations" paraphrase the original words, or even add interpretation, thus amplifying (but not contradicting) the meaning.

Every film enactment of biblical events falls somewhere on a similar spectrum: from a literal (word-for-word) depiction, to a dynamic equivalent, to a non-literal paraphrase. In the case of *The Chosen*, it would be fair to characterize it as beyond paraphrase to an "amplified version." Some would use this byline under it: *Based on a True Story*.

Such "non-literal," *historical fiction* relies on artistic license, and can cause discomfort which is understandable. If that is true for you, check out the videos by Dallas entitled: *Can you trust The Chosen?* (tinyurl.com/trust-the-chosen), as well as an interview with Jonathan Roumie, (tinyurl.com/roumie-interview), who portrays Jesus. These videos convey their perspective and may prove helpful.

We regularly point out what happened versus plausible speculation from *The Chosen*. Ultimately, *The Chosen* is a TV show, and the Bible is the only media inspired by God, given to inform us of the truth and the way things happened. Film brings supportive context and three-dimensional color to the two-dimensional writing on the page.

Dallas' heartfelt, well-achieved mission (see page 17) is why we vigorously support *The Chosen* and have developed *The Chosen Study*.

Background Notes:

More Notes:

Leader's Notes

The Chosen Vision: Dallas and his team share the goal of *reaching a billion people with the message of Jesus.* Our "loaves and fish" effort joins their far-reaching aspirations by **helping study leaders facilitate discussions about Jesus with everyone we know, and to see people grow into and as Christ followers.**

If you're on the fence about leading, consider Jesus' challenge to Andrew in Episode 8 of Season One about traveling through the hated Samaritan territory, a place considered unclean and dangerous: *Did you join me for safety reasons?*

So, you're interested in leading a Chosen Study? Here's what to do:

Gather a Core Team

The Chosen Study Team is a small group with a big purpose.
Draw together a core group made up of those who have seen something "different" in Jesus and want others to experience that difference. The team meets together regularly (shoot for weekly) to support the group process and pray. They plan, oversee the food, and invite friends and family to join in. This team can take on the following roles:

–***The Group Leader*** oversees the group's study and discussion process and seeks to foster one-on-one friendship evangelism and discipleship within the group. We encourage the Group Leader to model servant/ leadership within the group and to send out weekly emails.

–***The Prayer Team Promoter*** finds ways to support the Study in prayer.

–***The Meal Organizer*** oversees the food. See *Resources* at the website for theme potluck sign-up sheets. Meal Organizers can also keep in touch during the week with group emails. (The first meal will likely be something like a pizza night instead of a planned potluck.)

–**Child Care Helper** for younger families who need such help to come.

–**Set-Up/Sign-Up/Name Tag/Greeter** should be designated, especially for larger groups. For the people who may not feel comfortable at first, you'll want to extend hospitality and friendship from the start.

–**"Tech Person"** to oversee film presentation and casting to the TV.

–**Small Group Facilitators** (for larger studies—eight or more) oversee their group. **It is best to sit around small tables with just four to six others** (and best to separate spouses), rotating members weekly.

–**Day-Long or Weekend Event Organizer** (see page 15 and the website).

FYI: There are two series. **The Chosen Series** that follows *The Chosen* and **The Bible Series** which includes other film and passage selections from the Gospels and various books of Scripture. (See page 158 and the website for these options.)

Be Inclusive of Everyone

Who to invite? Everyone who is open to come: The religious, the doubters, the non-religious, the seekers—you name it. This is to be a fun, interactive place that values and respects everyone.

We hope group members share differences of opinion and viewpoints from all over the spiritual map. We're glad for that. Each person brings their own background. We're not here to judge. We love to stir up discussion and hear unaccustomed perspectives. As Jesus said to Simon in episode 7: *Get used to different!*

Sharing and Prayer: To respect where people are spiritually, encourage believers to **avoid insider-type sharing**—which can characterize typical Bible study groups. (Also, prayer should primarily take place before you come/after you leave, not during group time.) A Chosen Study is a **skeptic- and seeker-friendly outreach group** for mutual learning, and to develop deeper friendships both inside and outside the group context.

Get the Word Out

Direct Invitation: Yes, we still do that, right?! Indeed, it is by far the most effective means.

Email Invitation: Get the word out quickly by sending a link to the trailer, website, and a flyer attachment.

Text Invitation: Send out a photo, or better yet, a digital photo (JPG) of your flyer, and an active link to the trailer and website.

Flyers: Contact us at our website to receive sample flyers in MS Word that you can adapt and print or make up your own to hand out.

Create a Facebook Event and **Church Announcements** to the masses.

Once started, keep inviting. New people can binge watch to catch up!

Plan for Food

Our studies seek to connect us to God AND to each other. What better way to bring people together than by sharing food and conversation? We encourage starting with a meal, potluck or, at least, finger food. The role of overseeing the meals is a tremendous service to the group.

Lead/Facilitate the Group

You can begin small—with just one friend, one-on-one, or gather a group. Pray, invite, read, and underline the key points on pages 8-15 and 143-150. The leader's notes along the way, are for both current and future leaders to gain confidence in how to facilitate their groups.

Multiply Your Efforts—through small/large (8+) group combos

Combining small groups within a larger group: When a group starts off large or grows larger—*to eight or more*—the larger size presents unique opportunities. Small groups provide a *depth* of intimacy that allows members to participate more. Larger group interaction can then draw out the best insights from the small group discussions to offer a *breadth* of give-and-take sharing.

This combination **provides for two (shorter) discussion times**, with the best of both dynamics, and gives group leaders the role of a "dialogical" (two-way), not "monological" (one-way), teacher. After each small group time, the leader brings together the larger group for a "check-in" to highlight what was discussed within the small groups.

A small/large group combination **offers a chance for the core team to facilitate the smaller groups**. The goal is to foster a guided conversation. This, likewise, is true for a large group leader on a larger scale. Quality, dialogical teaching brings a soft touch to the group sharing, by focusing on the best insights gleaned from the small groups.

Larger groups thus **provide discipleship opportunities** for group members to step into the role of small group facilitators, as part of the core Chosen Study team. The goal is to help equip an increasing number of these leaders to multiply their outreach efforts in the lives of others. The challenge during the group time is to keep up the pace.

If you're currently a group member with such aspirations, feel free to study through the guide notes, go through the website and look for an opportunity to join a team, or to start your own Chosen Study!

For Leader Support: thechosenstudy.org/join

The website's primary purpose is to equip current and future leaders to make disciples and provide a community of discipleship for those using *The Chosen* for outreach and growth. *How can we serve you?*

Eight Group Ground Rules to Enhance Your Experience

1. *The Leader* is a **facilitator** of discussion, guiding the group through questions rather than statements. He or she is responsible to **prepare for and oversee group interaction** and to **help with outreach.**

2. *The Guide* makes for a valuable personal study but is especially set up to help **current and future leaders** facilitate watching, study, and discussion in one-to-one, and in small/large group settings.

3. *Prior Preparation* though not discouraged, is not expected. We do, however, have a **Home Reflection** time for post-Study follow-up.

4. *Each Group Member* "owns the group," and is thus seen as a key contributor of comments and questions. **Talkative members** should defer to others and **quiet members**, speak out. *The conversation engagement around the circle should look like a pinball machine!*

5. *Group Focus* is controlled by its purpose. *The Chosen* Study allows the episode and Scripture passage to **govern the discussion**, rather than Bible commentaries or cross referencing. Tangents are to be avoided or at least "tabled," until after the group meeting is over.

6. *Personal Growth* from studying Jesus is our goal. Such growth naturally includes a **focus on humility** and **child-like faith**.

7. *Group Growth* happens as **friendships form and deepen**. Members should see themselves as more than just a study group, but as a community where consistency, accountability, self-disclosure, empathy, and reaching out to others are key characteristics.

8. *Avoid making "guest appearances."* Don't let *stay-at-home feelings* or distractions dictate whether you come. **Commit to attend** every meeting. Take this gathering seriously—for you and for others.
Fight "those feelings" and the distractions by <u>signing this challenge</u>:

Unless out-of-town or near death's door, I'll be there: _____

Eight Don'ts of Leading Group Discussions

You're NOT a teacher, you're *a facilitator*. To lead a highly productive group discussion, start with what NOT to do and you're halfway there!

1. **Don't answer your own questions.** Otherwise, the group will look to you as "the teacher" rather than "the facilitator." You're not just the questioner. You should participate like any member, but don't be the first one to answer your own question.

2. **Don't over-talk.** Groups with an overtalkative leader will often sit back—in boredom! 90% of what we hear we forget, but 90% of what we say, we remember. So, your goal is to get your group talking. Get them remembering. Get them learning.

3. **Don't be afraid of silence.** Silence may mean you need to rephrase the question, but if you "bail out your group" when silent, you set a bad precedent. To exercise patience, count in your head from 100 to 0 before answering—then, only if you must. Oh, yes, they'll talk!

4. **Don't be content with just one answer.** For every written question feel free to ask a follow-up question or two, like: "Does anyone else have a thought?" This allows several people to respond.

5. **Don't expect group members to respond with an answer each time.** They'll be tempted to look straight at you solely, especially when the group is new. Instead, you want them talking to each other, so you don't have to be the "discussion hub" (see page 150).

6. **Don't reject an answer as wrong.** Respond to questionable answers by asking, "How did you come to that conclusion?" or "There's probably a difference of opinion here. Does anyone else have another way of looking at this?" Be affirming to everyone.

7. **Don't be afraid of controversy.** Different opinions are a good thing.

8. **Don't allow the group to end late.** If the discussion proves fruitful, end on time. Don't let the group drag on, but for those who choose to stay, give opportunity to discuss the issue in more depth.

Eight Do's of Leading Group Discussions

You don't need to be an expert or trained teacher to lead a discussion group. Your role is that of a **facilitator**, one who guides the group into a productive conversation that centers on the episodes' and studies' main points. It's an honor to be able to serve your group in this way.

1. **Bring along your own curiosity and have fun with it.** Good start!

2. **Pace the study.** It's the leader's responsibility to both start and end on time. Keep up a flexible pace with one eye on the clock and the other on the content. There may be more questions than you have time for; so, if necessary, skip some questions. Press ahead!

3. **Give members the chance to study on their own.** They are free to do so—or not. There is no expectation of prior preparation.

4. **Have the Scripture passage read aloud.** Ask a member to read. Some may feel uncomfortable reading in public, so don't make "surprise assignments," unless you know they're willing to do so.

5. **Be on alert for over talkative people.** Someone who over-talks can squeeze the life out of a group. If this is a problem, engage with the group member after the meeting, and enlist their help to join you in the goal of getting everyone involved in the discussion.

6. **Involve everyone, more or less equally.** Sit across from quiet people to draw them out, and next to talkative people to make less eye contact. If helpful, go around the circle with a question.

7. **Keep the discussion on track by avoiding tangents.** Tangents may seem important but can hurt purposeful discussion, leading the group to talk about less important things. "Important tangents" provide opportunities for conversation outside the group's time.

8. **Conduct a discussion first with general, then specific questions.** Your goal is NOT to get into one-and-done responses; rather, your goal is to start an engaging dialogue with several people responding to a particular question in a back-and-forth way (see next page).

Monological vs. Dialogical Interaction

If tables (small round or rectangle) are available, they are preferred for the meals and for group study (of ideally four to six participants each).

Dialogical interaction engages wide-ranging participation. Such give-and-take discussion sparked by the *table leader* and the *up-front leader* is desired. **Interaction from a leader's question is visualized below:**

Inferior Monological Interaction   Superior Dialogical Interaction

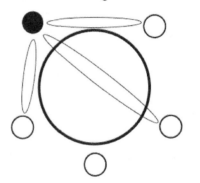 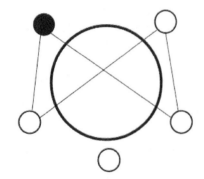

Small/Larger Group Combination—Can Work with Eight or More

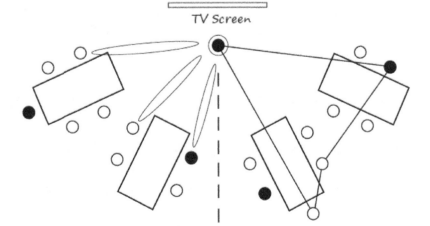

Dialogical leading *facilitates interaction* among your group members, and limits *brokering their discussion* seen above. As a leader you can participate, but your goal is to get others talking. 90% of what you say they'll forget, but 90% of what you get them to say, they'll remember!

Leader's Notes: What applies most to you and your group?

-
-
-
-
-
-
-
-
-
-
-
-
-
-
-
-
-

Your Chosen Group: Names, info., prayer concerns, etc.

-

-

-

-

-

-

-

-

-

-

-

-

-

-

-

-

Your Chosen Group: Names, info., prayer concerns, etc.

-
-
-
-
-
-
-
-
-
-
-
-
-
-
-

Note: For a sign-up sheet to print off, see the website under *Resources*.

Leader's Notes:

Our Mission: What We're About

The Chosen Study combines film depiction with Scripture study in a welcoming and interactive experience for all: observers... skeptics... learners... seekers... followers, who WATCH > DISCUSS > RELATE together the Most Audacious Story ever told.

Our Executive Leadership Team: What We Do

We work with Chosen Study Leaders, helping them succeed at gathering people, creating a friendly place and a compelling means to talk about Jesus.

Back to Front, Left to Right:
Bill Ditewig, Dietrich Gruen, Bill & Teresa Syrios and Cathy & Don Baker

Our Invitation: Start a Group–Join the Team–Zoom with Us

Do you have some loaves and fish to bring to this endeavor? We are looking for those who have seen "the Jesus difference" and are interested in exploring how to spread that difference around the world using *The Chosen Study*. If that sounds like you, contact us: thechosenstudy.org/join or facebook.com/thechosenstudy.

More Notes

Order Guides (with volume discounts): thechosenstudy.org/order

The Chosen Study: **Season One,** focuses on Simon, Matthew, Andrew, Nicodemus, and Mary Magdalene as they encounter Jesus. This guide, based on the hugely popular show, *The Chosen*, will give you and your group an in-depth appreciation of their unexpected changes of fortune in getting to know him.

The Chosen Study: **Season Two,** guides you and your group into Act Two of Jesus' life and ministry with his followers unsure of where all this is going.

Here we meet the remaining disciples, such as Nathanael, who is despondent over a career in shambles, only to be given a new vocation by Jesus. Besides him, there are a host of others with physical, mental, and emotional infirmities, even demon-possession that, up to now, have been impossible to overcome.

The Chosen Study: **Season Three,** will begin with *The Messengers*—which first aired in theaters before Christmas, 2021. It then picks up where season two ended, with the famous *Sermon on the Mount.*

Chosen seasons four through seven

We know little of what's coming, other than season six will focus on Jesus' crucifixion and season seven, his resurrection. Otherwise, stay tuned for many more gospel stories!

Special one-time Chosen event

The Messengers, Christmas Special: This episode can be used as a *come-one-come-all event* for your group or church before Christmas. Some are more open spiritually around Christmas. Watching and discussing this episode could act as a winter-quarter (January) kickoff for a new Chosen group. To access it, see: tinyurl.com/chosen-messengers

Further encouragement

The Chosen: 40 Days with Jesus provides a new devotional for each season to extend your experience throughout the week. You can space it out to follow a five-a-week schedule. Order at Amazon or bookstores.

Divide the 40 devotional readings into five readings per week.

Bible Series Guide

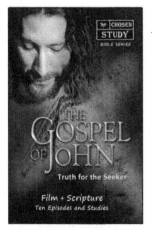

We're spoiled by *The Chosen*, but there are other quality, biblical movies, and *Jesus films* out there. Here's one that we are working on:

The John Study is a ten-week series based on a film entitled *The Life of Jesus*. This three-hour movie is a word-for-word portrayal of John's Gospel from the *Good News Bible* translation.

Watch the movie: tinyurl.com/the-john-study

Manuscript Bible Study

We use four-color BIC pens to colorfully study biblical texts in the *Mark-It-Up* style.

The *M-I-U format* is based on something more in-depth called *manuscript Bible study*.

Such study is done on 8 ½ x 11" sheets. The text is set out with margins as seen in this example from the first 15 verses of Mark's Gospel.

For more info and to access downloadable manuscripts: manuscriptbiblestudy.com.

How to Lead and Promote a Chosen Study

The Chosen Study really began on May 28, 2021 with a Zoom call led by Bill Syrios with some gifted Bible study leaders. Get in on that call here: tinyurl.com/how-to-lead. Also, learn to lead in the process!

The Chosen Study Zoom calls continue, led Bill Syrios with those who became colleagues. These calls, on June 4 and 11, 2021 focus on promoting your Chosen group to others. See: tinyurl.com/how-to-promote.

Final Thoughts!

Made in the USA
Monee, IL
14 January 2023

25131599R00089